THE
FIRST
COAST

Heritage

COOKBOOK

Written by JEFFREY SPEAR

Designed by PATRICK CARTER & JEFFREY SPEAR
Photography by VINCE LUPO

IN GOOD
···· PRESS ····
TASTE

IN GOOD TASTE PRESS
PO Box 51291
Jacksonville, Florida 32240
www.igtpress.com

Published 2013

Printed in the United States

Design by Patrick Carter and Jeffrey Spear

Photography by Vince Lupo

ISBN 13: 978-0-9889191-0-5

TABLE OF CONTENTS

....

For Hortense Spear
I will never forget.

DEDICATION

TO THOSE WHO COOK... AND LOVE

This book is written at a time in American history when food is embraced as entertainment; a voyeuristic compulsion evidenced by the glut of food-oriented programming on television as well as the seemingly endless number of cooking and tasting events that have popped up in every corner of the country. What started with Julia Child in modest form has exploded to staggering proportions.

Culinary trends are also leaning towards regional cooking and locally produced ingredients - understanding the nuances and specialties that have emerged from geographically specific food producing regions, including their distinctive ethnic neighborhoods and communities.

While this book acknowledges and caters to the dynamics outlined above, it is written for readers who are eager to learn more about the culinary heritage that started along the Florida peninsula so many years ago. It is also for cooks who find the understanding and preparation of food a genuinely satisfying endeavor.

Lastly, it is for individuals who understand that gathering at the dinner table with friends and family and the sharing of food is an act of undeniable generosity and love.

INTRODUCTION

A TIME LONG GONE

The northeast corner of the Floridian peninsula, including St. Augustine and Jacksonville, is the region in North America that was first settled by Europeans in 1565. More than 400 years later, and as part of an advertising campaign sponsored by the Jacksonville Chamber of Commerce [1983] in recognition of this historical legacy, the region was creatively named "Florida's First Coast."

The First Coast Heritage Cookbook investigates and celebrates the foodways of tribes and communities that lived and cooked along Florida's First Coast from 14,000 BC [the time archeologists tell us evidence of human habitation first appears] to 1821 [when Florida becomes a U.S. Territory].

During this time, settlement was not the result of just one group of individuals arriving from a single homeland. To the contrary, the people who are responsible for establishing the villages and towns in this region can be grouped broadly into five culturally unrelated and distinctive groups: Indigenous Indian, Spanish, French, British, and African.

Of particular interest are the uniquely different paths, as well as motivating influences, that brought each of these groups to the region.

The indigenous Indian populations settled as a result of tribal migrations that took place over thousands of years, starting from the Siberian peninsula and traveling across the land bridge that connected it to North America. From there, their wanderings transversed the continent, establishing communities along the way. Eventually, nomadic tribes made their way down and across the continent and settled in the area centered on the waterway now recognized as the St. John's River.

It was not until the intrusion of European explorers that things began to dramatically change. Although approximately 200,000 members of the Saturiba tribe had managed to prosper in this region for thousands of years, the diseases carried by outsiders led to their extinction. In very short time, and without weapons or violent conflict, settlers effectively destroyed a society that had endured for nearly 500 generations.

The Spanish explorers came to the Florida peninsula as part of an extensive effort to discover, conquer, and colonize new lands for their king and country. Sailing from harbors in Hispaniola [Haiti] that had been established by Christopher Columbus in 1492, exploration and settlement took place along the Floridian peninsula's coastal territories and spread as far North as the Chesapeake Bay. The names of the expedition leaders we remember most from these times are Columbus, de Soto, and Menendez. Most notably, we remember Juan Ponce de Leon, the Spanish captain who named this territory "La Florida" on April 2, 1513.

As with the Spanish, the French were also attempting to establish colonies in the New World. In the spring of 1562, Captain Jean Ribault established New France along the eastern coast of North America in the place that is now South Carolina. During this time, he also surveyed the mouth of the St. John's River. Recognizing the strategic benefits this harbor had to offer, a second French expedition lead by Captain René de Laudonniere was dispatched. Under this second command, the French established a short-lived presence with the founding of Fort Caroline on April 22, 1564.

The British were also colonizing in North America. While their settlements between Virginia and New Hampshire were amongst their first, actions made it clear that colonization was not limited to these northern lands. In 1586 the British attacked, but failed to overtake, St. Augustine. While tensions and repeated skirmishes continued, it wasn't until 1763 that the British took possession of Florida. Twenty years later, however, it would be returned to Spain.

The first Africans that came to North America were among the earliest non-natives to set foot in Florida. They were part of the explorer fleets that sailed in this region, arriving with Columbus in 1492 and subsequently landing on the Floridian peninsula with Juan Ponce in 1513.

That being said, the majority of Africans arrived in North America between 1710 and 1810, coming primarily from tribal villages along the West Coast of Africa. Unlike the Spanish, French, or British, they were brought to this new territory by force and worked as slaves. They were property. While all of these individuals are long gone, their culinary influence endures. By recognizing the advances in food production, cooking methodologies, and new ingredients that arrived with each wave of settlers, we can see how dramatically the foodways along the First Coast have changed.

Prior to the first footfall of European explorers on the Floridian peninsula, many of the foods we are familiar with and enjoy today were nowhere to be found. Ingredients we take for granted, including beef, pork, lamb, apples, cherries, peanuts, peaches, watermelons, okra, oranges, and potatoes simply did not exist in North America - they were all introduced from other lands.

When the indigenous Indians populated the Floridian peninsula, they relied entirely on native fruits, vegetables, abundant seafood, and wild game. While beans, corn, pumpkin, and squash were at the core of their diet, the region provided a wide variety of foodstuffs upon which their communities thrived.

The 1500s represents a significant change in foodways throughout the world, owing much to the transportation and growing trade of foodstuffs across oceans and between countries.

In other regions, the Spanish had already been transporting and trading foods - most notably potatoes and chocolate from Maya and Aztec tribes living in Mesoamerica. While establishing settlements along the Floridian peninsula, they also introduced pigs, potatoes, citrus, and peaches.

While the French were recognized as having the greatest influence on foodways throughout Europe in the 16th, 17th and 18th centuries, their expeditions to the First Coast did not reflect this accomplishment. Although they brought provisions, the settlers were primarily military personnel. They had not been trained to farm, and in some cases, did not know how to use a gun for hunting.

As supplies ran short, and without the ability to collect or grow sufficient quantities of food on their own, they were forced to rely upon local Indian tribes for nearly everything they ate.

The British were more fortunate and managed to establish colonies with greater ease in the regions extending from Virginia to New England. By the time their campaigns for southerly territories proved successful, and they possessed St. Augustine and the Floridian peninsula, their colonial foodways were well established.

As with all of the other explorers and settlers who came to North America, the British learned and embraced foodways from native Indians. Over time, they added to this diet with ingredients including white potatoes, rum, wheat, barley, beef, apples, and cherries.

During voyages from Africa, and finding that the slaves would reject unfamiliar foods provided onboard ships, transporters were forced to carry African ingredients. This allowed African food-ways to establish a foothold in the New World.

Additionally, once the Africans were settled, they were forced to survive on whatever foods they could forage or grow on their own along with the meager ingredients and off-cuts of meat that were provided by their "masters." The combination of their African heritage, transported foodstuffs, and learning to survive on the discarded or lower quality ingredients obtained from the "big house" provided the foundation for much of what we now identify as southern cooking.

Of course, there were many other cultures and ethnicities that contributed to the settlement of the First Coast - many of their contributions becoming most apparent during migrations that took place in the 19th and 20th centuries. For the purposes of this book, however, and considering that its framework is the culinary influence and foodways that existed prior to 1821, it is appropriate to focus upon the Indigenous Indian, French, Spanish, British, and African settlers.

ABOUT THE RECIPES

American Cookery, written by Amelia Simmons in 1796, was the first cookbook penned by an American. It relied on English cooking traditions [Simmons lived in the northern colonies, most likely somewhere in New York] and was the first to be influenced by the foodways and culinary contributions made by native North American Indians. Before this time, and aside from cookbooks published in Europe with European recipes, very little written evidence exists regarding ingredients, recipes, or cooking preferences in North America.

The First Coast Heritage Cookbook is a collection of recipes influenced by the ingredients and foodways of the Indigenous Indians as well as the Spanish, French, and British settlers who inhabited the First Coast. It also recognizes the undeniable influence that enslaved Africans had on the culinary landscape in this region and throughout the South.

OLD RECIPES MADE NEW

While every effort has been made to be historically accurate in the editorial portions of this book, it would be unrealistic, and in some cases impossible, for today's cook to accurately reproduce the dishes prepared so long ago. Ingredients such as Woolly Mammoth and Giant Land Tortoise are extinct; the Florida Black Bear is an endangered species; and the idea of cooking squirrel, possum, and especially rat would be unpalatable to all but the most adventurous of cooks.

In addition, meals prepared thousands of years ago, and even just a few hundred years ago, were eaten strictly for survival. Unlike today's "foodies" who derive great pleasure and entertainment value from the dishes they prepare, the idea of cooking food as a relaxing pastime in the 16th, 17th and even 18th centuries, except amongst royalty and the wealthiest of society, would be considered ludicrous.

From a cooking perspective, the use of open fires, a hearth, and/or coals as a heat source was common and utilized by all of the explorers and settlers mentioned in this book. In today's kitchens, however, cooks have access to sophisticated stoves and ovens and incorporate outdoor cooking and grilling as an option, not a necessity.

Additionally, modern cooks have the benefit of a wide range of herbs and spices; ingredients that were rare, expensive, and available primarily to royalty and the wealthiest of households back in the 16th, 17th, and 18th centuries. To prepare foods without these ingredients today, while historically accurate, would be disappointing to say the least.

Lastly, the idea behind these recipes is to give the cook a greater appreciation of the ingredients and foodways that make up such a strong part of our Floridian heritage - to give added relevance to ingredients such as pork, corn, peaches, potatoes, and sugar that were new and special so many years ago. To insist upon open fires, minimally spiced or altogether bland recipes and questionable ingredients would not provide the level of enjoyment this book is meant to deliver.

FROM GENERATION TO GENERATION

To say the recipes in this book have historical merit would be a significant overstatement. While they do feature ingredients that were important factors in the survival and foodways of the tribes, explorers, and settlers who lived along the First Coast so many years ago, they are simply a collection of recipes that have been found in various Floridian history books and regional family archives while conducting research.

It is important to note, however, that the measures, proportions, and cooking tools used hundreds of years ago are quite different from those of today. In addition, some of the recipes uncovered would be considered far too bland or even unpalatable if cooked to the original author's specifications.

Accordingly, each and every recipe in this book has been tested, then revised and updated to include a properly described ingredients list and fully functional cooking instructions that align with modern cooking practices and taste

preferences. It is, after all, the goal of this book to provide you, the reader, with a successful and enjoyable cooking experience steeped in history and cultural significance.

SUCCESSES AND FAILURES

There is very little evidence, other than clues found in archaeological records, to tell us what the indigenous Indians were eating thousands of years ago. Even as recently as a few hundred years ago, Indian tribes did not maintain written records of their foodways.

From a European perspective, explorers had more on their minds than finding some fabulous recipe to impress their friends, family, and neighbors. While they did identify and transport a large number of intriguing and exotic ingredients, and found great riches from the trading of these foodstuffs, their focus was on the acquisition of territory, precious metals, and other such treasures. At the same time, they were also fending off perilous advances from other colonizing nations.

As such, content for this book relied heavily on evidence found in ship's manifests and scholarly historical writings - documents that go no further than to identify what foods were being collected, transported, and consumed. While they occasionally provide colorful descriptions, any indication of exactly how the foods were prepared is, to great degree, glossed over.

On top of this, when definitions of ingredients and some indication of proportion or measurement are documented, they tend to be vague - certainly not up to the standards we expect in cookbooks today.

Needless to say, there was a fair amount of guesswork and "fudging" of recipes based on anecdotal information as well as more contemporary versions of similar recipes.

While all of the recipes provided in this book are, after numerous attempts, quite complete and ready for your enjoyment, you may still wish to make modifications of your own - especially if you have grown up in the northeast corner of Florida and have enjoyed comparable dishes - either those passed down from generation to generation or in some of the wonderful, similarly inspired restaurants in the region.

DEFINITIONS, WEIGHTS & MEASURES

Before you start cooking, it is important to confirm certain definitions, weights, and measures.

Eggs are always large; butter is always unsalted; and flour, unless specified, is all-purpose.

Ingredients such as beans, greens, and squash are available in numerous varieties and can be easily interchanged. While their flavor, texture, and color may vary somewhat, there are plenty of alternatives.

Lima beans, black-eyed beans, red beans, kidney beans, and black beans can be substituted for one another. Collard greens, kale, spinach, and chard are equally interchangeable. Pumpkin, butternut, kabocha, acorn, and carnival are all delicious varieties of squash.

If you find that any of the ingredients are unfamiliar, using the Internet for more detailed explanations is an excellent start. The same goes for purchasing unfamiliar ingredients that may not be available in local supermarkets or specialty stores.

While the recipes in this book have shunned historically viable and frequently used ingredients such as bear, deer, rabbit, turtle, snake, and possum, these foodstuffs are easily found and can be purchased online.

Regarding measures, tablespoons are abbreviated as T, whereas teaspoons appear as tsp. Cups are C, pounds appear as lb. and ounces as oz.

Hopefully everything else is clearly written and fully described. If not, just imagine what it must have been like for the first settlers in this part of the world. No electric appliances. No refrigeration. No supermarkets. If you wanted to eat, you grew it, hunted it, or foraged for it in the neighborhood. You'll do just fine.

THE EARLIEST RECORD OF HUMAN HABITATION ALONG THE FLORIDA PENINSULA DATES BACK TO 14,000 BC. PALEO-INDIAN AND SUBSEQUENT INDIAN POPULATIONS FLOURISHED IN THIS REGION AS HUNTERS AND GATHERERS, RELYING ON WHATEVER EDIBLE PLANT AND ANIMAL LIFE WAS AVAILABLE.

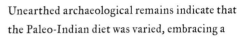

As a matter of orientation, evidence indicates that the surroundings were significantly different from what we find today. As a result of polar freezing, coastal waters had receded, creating a significantly larger land mass. Additionally, the Florida peninsula looked more like a drier and sparsely foliated version of the contemporary African veldt, as opposed to the richly foliated landscape along the First Coast today.

The animal life that roamed this region was varied. From a human perspective, camels, horses, and bison were reasonably sized, making hunting, transportation, and preparation of carcasses a manageable task. Of course, there were giants lumbering around as well, including the Woolly Mammoth, Giant Land Tortoise, Giant Armadillos, and Mastodons. While the yield of culinary ingredients from any one of these creatures was sizeable and would cater a feast of massive proportions, the task of bringing one down was a bit more challenging.

Unearthed archaeological remains indicate that the Paleo-Indian diet was varied, embracing a variety of plants, land and sea creatures. Meals were prepared based solely on the need to survive and what had been successfully hunted or collected on a given day. While the notion of Giant Land Tortoise in Garlic Sauce or a Woolly Mammoth Casserole is appealing, it is important to note that these ingredients, along with many other foodstuffs from this period, have since become extinct. Even the horses that ran wild during this ancient time are gone. The ones we see today are descendants of herds imported by European settlers just a few hundred years ago. Clearly, the idea of recipes from this era is ludicrous.

By the time the Spaniards "discovered" Florida in 1513, the territory was populated with approximately 200,000 indigenous Indians. The Saturiba tribe [speaking a dialect known as Timucuan] dominated the First Coast with settlements as far north as Georgia and southward to St. Augustine. These were the people who greeted the Spanish [and the French] upon arrival.

It is interesting to note that the Spaniards called the people "cimarrones," meaning free people, because they would not allow themselves to be dominated. The word gained traction and, by the mid-1800s, locals had distorted the name, referring to all Florida natives as "Seminoles."

Hospitality was extended by the Indians to the newly arrived European visitors in much the same way we treat guests in our own homes today. Drinks were offered, meals were served, and tips about the good foods available in the region were shared.

The typical welcoming, social, and ceremonial drink was a black tea made from Cassina [a wild holly plant] that is rich in caffeine - considerably stronger than the coffees and teas we enjoy today. Visitors were also treated to a one-pot soup made from corn and venison called "sofki."

Over time, the Europeans would also make sofki. In their hands, however, the recipe evolved into a heartier stew that might include rabbit, crab, turkey, or fish. There is evidence that newly imported bananas and potatoes also found their way into the dish.

Food preparation relied heavily on corn, squash, and beans - a culinary foundation frequently referred to as the "Three Sisters." In addition, fish and shellfish were important dietary staples. Meats were typically grilled or smoked over coals. One-pot stews and soups were prepared and kept hot for consumption throughout the day.

When it came to processed grains and flours, any number of seeds would be ground or milled and subsequently cooked into porridges or stews and baked into bread. One of the more widely used ingredients for making bread was coontie [arrow root]. The Indians would extract and dry a starch from the stems of this plant and subsequently use it to make an orange-hued bread.

In spite of an absence of written history, or any tangible indication of note-keeping that would provide insight to the recipes the Indians embraced prior to the arrival of European settlers, there is still a rich archaeological record of foodways during the Seminole years which includes an extensive list of ingredients the Indians consumed.

Some of the more familiar are:

ALLIGATOR	HICKORY NUTS	RACCOON
BEAR	MANATEE	RAT
CLAMS	MUSCADINE GRAPES	SWAMP CABBAGE
CONCH	ONION	SNAILS
CRAB	OYSTERS	SNAKE
DEER	PERSIMMONS	SQUIRREL
DRAGON ROOT	POSSUM	SUNFLOWER SEEDS
DUCK	PUMPKIN	TORTOISE
FROG	RABBIT	TURKEY

Over time, and in many cases as a matter of survival, the foodways of the Indians were fully embraced by the Europeans. Hunting, catching, and preparing fish, alligator, squirrel, possum, raccoon, rabbit, and bear were all exotic culinary experiences for the newly arrived settlers. At the same time, the Indians were introduced to ingredients that were being imported from other lands including pork, bananas, and sweet potatoes. When the Spanish introduced peaches to the Indians, they took to them immediately. In fact, settlers who arrived somewhat later assumed the Indians had cultivated the fruit and introduced it to the Europeans.

While relations were peaceful, and the indigenous Indians tolerated the comings and goings of European intruders, the sad reality is that the introduction of European diseases and violent conflict with invaders would completely destroy their way of life - one that had been enjoyed for more than 500 generations. For now, the best we can do is to remember the undeniably important role these early inhabitants played in the history of Florida and enjoy the meals they inspired.

INDIAN CORN CHOWDER SOFKI*

Serves 8

INGREDIENTS

3/4 lbs bacon, cut into
1/2" pieces

2 C onion, diced

4 C yellow corn

2 C hominy

1 1/2 lbs pork butt, cut into
3/4" squares

salt and pepper, to taste

DIRECTIONS

In a Dutch oven, fry the bacon until cooked but not crunchy. Remove from pan and reserve. Using the residual bacon fat, sauté onion until soft. Add 2 C of the corn and all of the hominy, cooking further until carmelized.

Transfer the corn mixture to a blender and liquefy, adding water a little at a time, as needed. Set aside.

Using the same pot, brown the pork on all sides, then add enough water to cover. Bring to a boil, then simmer for approximately 1 1/2 hours until tender.

Remove the pork from the broth, allowing the meat to cool slightly, then shred.

Return the corn puree, shredded pork, bacon and remaining 2 cups of whole yellow corn to the pot. Simmer for 20 minutes.

Add salt and pepper, to taste.

Serve immediately with thick crusty bread.

SOFKI IS THE INDIAN NAME GIVEN TO A STEW MADE WITH HOMINY AND VENISON. THE INDIANS USED THIS DISH, AS WELL AS MANY OTHERS, AS A WAY OF EXTENDING HOSPITALITY TO HUNGRY VISITORS.

PUMPKIN SOUP

Serves 8

INGREDIENTS

1 1/2 T butter

1 C carrot, coarsely chopped

1 C celery, coarsely chopped

1 C onion, coarsely chopped

2 cloves garlic, minced

2 bay leaves

5 C chicken broth

3 C pumpkin,* peeled, seeded, coarsely chopped

1 banana, ripe, coarsely chopped

3/4 C coconut milk

1/4 C sweetened condensed milk

1 whole clove

1 tsp nutmeg

1/2 tsp cinnamon

1/2 tsp coriander

1/2 tsp sage

1/4 t allspice

1/4 tsp curry

salt and pepper

1/4 C cilantro, chopped, for garnish

DIRECTIONS

Melt butter in a large soup pot or Dutch oven. Add carrot, celery, onion, garlic and bay leaves and sauté for approximately 15 minutes or until soft.

Add all of the remaining ingredients, except for the cilantro, and bring to a boil. Immediately reduce heat and simmer until pumpkin is soft.

Remove bay leaves. In small batches, transfer the soup mixture to a blender and puree until smooth.

Season with salt and pepper, to taste.

Ladle into bowls, garnish with cilantro and serve.

* *If pumpkin is unavailable, try Kabocha or Butternut squash.*

BEAR HEAD HASH

Serves 8   [*See Photo - Page* 17]

INGREDIENTS

DIRECTIONS

3 T olive oil

1 onion, chopped

1 red bell pepper, seeded,
cut into 1/4-inch dice

1 green bell pepper, seeded,
cut into 1/4 inch dice

1/2 lb leftover beef, pork,
or chicken, fully cooked,
cut into 1/4-inch dice

2 lb potatoes, peeled, cut
into 1/4-inch dice

2 T chopped parsley

1/4 tsp cayenne

salt and pepper, to taste

8 eggs

Heat the oil in a large non-stick frying or sauté pan. Add the onion, red and green peppers and cook until soft, approximately 15 minutes. Add in the potatoes and meat followed by the parsley, cayenne, salt and pepper. Flatten the mixture into the pan, cooking 15 to 20 minutes longer, ensuring potatoes are fully cooked. Toss at least once while cooking, obtaining a crusty brownness to the meat and potatoes.

While the hash is cooking, prepare eggs [fried, poached, scrambled, etc.] to your liking.

Distribute the crusty hash equally onto eight plates; top with one portion of egg. Serve immediately.

Although bears are a protected species today, they were plentiful and considered a staple food source by Indians and European settlers. This dish was originally prepared using the animal's head. It would be cooked and stripped of its meat, then chopped and fried in fat along with vegetables and seasoning. While you could still make this recipe with bear meat that is legally harvested, this configuration allows you to use whatever protein you happen to have in the fridge.

BEAR HEAD HASH [*See recipe - pg 16*]

CATFISH & FENNEL STEW

Serves 8

INGREDIENTS

3 T olive oil, extra-virgin

1 C onion, finely diced

1 C fennel, coarsely diced
[set aside fronds for garnish]

6 garlic cloves, minced

2 tsp fresh thyme, finely
chopped

1 bay leaf

3 C fish stock

28 oz crushed tomatoes

1 C dry white wine

1/2 C dry sherry

2 C pumpkin, seeded, peeled
and cut into 1/2" pieces

6 oz tomato paste

Salt and pepper, to taste

1 1/2 lb catfish, cut into
1-inch pieces

DIRECTIONS

Heat the olive oil in a Dutch oven over medium heat. Add onion, fennel
and garlic and sauté until soft, about 5 minutes. Add thyme and bay
leaf and cook for 1 minute. Add stock, tomatoes, wine and sherry and
bring to boil. Reduce to a simmer, cover and cook for 20 minutes.

Add pumpkin, cooking until just tender. Stir in tomato paste, then
salt and pepper to taste. Add catfish, simmering until fully cooked,
about 5 minutes.

Can be served on its own with thick crusty bread or over white rice.
Garnish with fennel fronds.

CORNMEAL ENCRUSTED OYSTERS

Serves 6 - 8

INGREDIENTS

DIRECTIONS

24 oysters [best if freshly shucked]

1 1/2 cups yellow cornmeal

1/2 C flour

2 tsp salt

1/2 tsp cayenne pepper

1/2 tsp black pepper

1 C buttermilk

Preheat oven to 450°F.

Drain oysters completely.

In a shallow dish or pie plate, mix cornmeal, flour, salt, cayenne and pepper. Pour buttermilk into a separate bowl.

Dip the oysters into the buttermilk, then into the cornmeal, taking care not to build up too thick a crust. Place fully coated oysters onto a lightly oiled baking sheet. Bake* until golden brown on their bottoms, abut 10 minutes, then turn over and bake an additional 10 minutes.

Serve with SPICY COCKTAIL SAUCE

Frying the oysters in smoking hot vegetable oil works equally well.

SPICY COCKTAIL SAUCE

Serves 6 - 8

INGREDIENTS

DIRECTIONS

1/2 C ketchup

2 T lime juice, fresh squeezed

1 T prepared horseradish

Mix all of the ingredients together. Refrigerate for 2 hours before serving.

CORN & CRAB CASSEROLE

Serves 8

INGREDIENTS

4 T butter

1/4 C breadcrumbs

2 C corn kernels

1 red pepper, diced

4 T flour

1 1/2 C milk

4 eggs

1/2 lb gruyere cheese

pepper sauce, to taste

1 tsp salt

1 lb jumbo lump crab meat

DIRECTIONS

Preheat oven to 400° F.

Grease a 2 qt baking dish with butter. Pour in breadcrumbs, tilting the dish so that all sides are covered. Set aside.

Melt 1 T butter in a sauté pan. Add corn and diced peppers and cook until most of the moisture is removed and the vegetables begin to caramelize. Remove from heat and set aside.

Beat eggs in a large bowl and set aside.

Melt the remaining 3 T butter in a small saucepan. Whisk in flour to make a roux. Slowly add in milk, whisking constantly until the mixture thickens. Slowly whisk this mixture in with the eggs, a small amount at a time, whisking constantly. You don't want the hot sauce to cook the eggs. This should be slow and cautious process.

Once the sauce and eggs are fully combined, mix in the cheese, pepper sauce and salt followed by the corn and red peppers. When completely mixed, gently fold in the crab meat, taking care not to break up the lumps.

Pour this mixture into the prepared baking dish and place in the preheated oven. Reduce the temperature to 375°F and bake for approximately 30 - 40 minutes or until the dish is firm in the center and nicely browned.

Allow to rest for 15 minutes before serving.

CRAB & SWAMP CABBAGE SALAD

Serves 4 [*See Photo - Page 22*]

INGREDIENTS

1/2 C extra-virgin olive oil

2 T lemon juice, freshly squeezed

2 T lime juice, freshly squeezed

1 T honey

2 tsp kosher salt

Pinch black pepper

1 C hearts of palm, cut diagonally into 1/4-inch slices

8 oz crabmeat

1 T coarsely chopped cilantro

1 T julienned basil [chiffonade]

1 T julienned mint [chiffonade]

salt and pepper, to taste

4 oz arugula

2 oranges, supremed

DIRECTIONS

Make a dressing by whisking together the olive oil, lemon juice, lime juice, honey, salt and pepper. Place the hearts of palm in a bowl, pour in half of the dressing and mix. Cover and refrigerate for at least one hour. Use the remaining salad dressing to prepare the crabmeat and for serving.

In another bowl, mix the crabmeat, cilantro, basil, mint, salt, pepper and 1 tsp dressing. Toss gently until thoroughly mixed, taking care not to break up the crab.

To serve, divide the arugula evenly between 4 plates; top with hearts of palm followed by crab. Garnish with 4 orange supremes on each salad. Drizzle a little dressing over top.

CRAB & SWAMP CABBAGE SALAD [*See recipe - pg 21*]

TIMUCUA SALAD

Serves 12

INGREDIENTS

2 C baby lima beans*

2 C corn

1 lb. hearts of palm, sliced into 1/4 inch pieces

1 lb. tomatoes, diced

1 C red onion, minced

1/2 C cilantro, chopped

1/3 C olive oil

1 lime, juiced

Salt and pepper, to taste

DIRECTIONS

Place all of the ingredients in a large bowl, mixing thoroughly. Cover and place in refrigerator for at least 4 hours, allowing flavors to come together. Adjust seasoning as needed before serving.

* *Also good using black-eyed beans, red kidney beans and black beans.*

THE SABAL PALM IS THE STATE TREE OF FLORIDA. THE YOUNG PLANT [FROM WHICH THE HEARTS ARE EXTRACTED] LOOKS SOMEWHAT LIKE CABBAGE, HENCE THE NAME "SWAMP CABBAGE."

CORN PUDDING

Serves 8 - 12

INGREDIENTS

4 C milk, scalded

1/2 C corn meal

1/8 tsp salt

1/3 C molasses

1/2 C brown sugar

1/2 tsp ginger

1/2 tsp cinnamon

2 eggs

DIRECTIONS

Preheat the oven to 350° F.

In a saucepan, carefully heat milk just shy of boiling, stirring constantly. Slowly whisk in the corn meal, taking care to avoid lumps. Whisk in the salt, molasses, brown sugar, ginger and cinnamon. Continue cooking under low heat for approximately 20 minutes, stirring frequently, until thickened.

In a separate bowl, beat the eggs. Temper the eggs by slowly whisking in approximately one cup of the batter, then slowly whisk the egg mixture back into the batter.

Pour the batter into a greased 2-quart pan. Bake at 350° F for 60 minutes or until fully set.

Allow the pudding to cool for about 30 minutes. Serve warm with whipped cream.

MUSCADINE CHEESE CAKE

Serves 8 - 10

INGREDIENTS

DIRECTIONS

CRUST

1/3 C butter, melted

3 T sugar

1 1/4 C graham cracker
crumbs

CHEESE LAYER

8oz cream cheese, softened

1/3 cup sugar

2 eggs

1/4 tsp almond extract

CREAM LAYER

1 C sour cream

1 1/2 T sugar

1/2 tsp vanilla

FRUIT GLAZE*

2 C Muscadine grapes, seeds
removed

3 T sugar

2 T tapioca

Preheat the oven to 350° F.

Start by making the crust: Mix the butter, sugar and graham crumbs together. Press into the bottom and sides of a 9" spring form pan.

To make the cheese layer, beat the cream cheese, sugar, eggs and almond extract together until thoroughly mixed. Pour this mixture into the bottom of the pie crust and bake for 25 minutes. Allow to cool.

For the cream layer, mix together the sour cream, sugar and vanilla. Spread this mixture on top of baked layer and bake for an additional 10 minutes. Cool completely.

For the fruit glaze, place the grapes, sugar and tapioca in a blender until smooth. Allow the topping to rest for 10 minutes, then pour over the cheesecake.

Refrigerate for 6 hours or overnight before serving

Muscadine grapes have exceptionally thick skins. For the fruit glaze, you'll want to use a blender capable of liquefying them completely.

PEACH PIE

Serves 8

INGREDIENTS

DIRECTIONS

PIE CRUST

3/4 C shortening [Crisco]

1/4 C water, boiling

1 T milk

2 C flour, sifted

1 tsp salt

FILLING

8 peaches, ripe

1 C sugar

1 T flour

pinch of salt

vanilla ice cream

Preheat the oven to 425° F.

Make the dough: Put the shortening in a large bowl. Add boiling water and milk and, with a fork, cut and mix the ingredients until most of the liquid has been absorbed.

Mix in the flour and salt until you can form a ball with your hands. Divide the dough into two parts, one for the bottom crust and one for the top, and set aside.

Make the filling: Peel and slice the peaches and place in a large bowl. Mix in the sugar, flour and salt.

Assemble the pie: Roll out one dough ball for the bottom crust and place in a 9" pie plate. Pour in the peach mixture. Roll out the second dough ball to make the top crust. Pinch the top and bottom crusts together with a fork. Poke two or three holes in the top crust for venting.

Bake at 425° F for 20 minutes. Reduce heat to 375° F and bake for an additional 30-45 minutes. The pie should be golden brown and bubbling.

Serve with a scoop of vanilla ice cream.

 ALTHOUGH INTRODUCED BY THE SPANISH, THE INDIANS TOOK TO PEACHES SO COMPLETELY THAT THE FRUIT WAS BELIEVED INDIGENOUS.

SPANISH SETTLERS

THE SPANISH EXPLORERS, COMMANDED BY JUAN PONCE DE LEÓN, LANDED ON THE SOUTHEASTERN PENINSULAR COAST OF NORTH AMERICA ON APRIL 2, 1513. UPON ARRIVAL, THE TERRITORY WAS CLAIMED AS SPANISH TERRITORY AND GIVEN THE NAME "LA FLORIDA."

While hotly contested by the French and British in frequent and bloody attacks for years to come, the Spanish endured. That being said, as a result of treaties between warring nations, Florida was ceded to the British in 1763, returned to the Spanish in 1784, and finally turned over to the British, once and for all, in 1821.

While there are numerous accounts of these voyages, settlements, and conflicts, and we cannot overlook their historical significance, the culinary heritage attributed to the Spanish during this time, and especially in northeast Florida, is arguably far more remarkable.

To begin, it is essential to acknowledge the robust nature of Spanish explorations throughout the world. While in pursuit of land and treasure, these intrepid explorers were transporting and trading a surprisingly large volume of fruits, vegetables, spices, and livestock between South and Central America and Spain along the way.

The Conquistadores, after encounters with the Aztecs in Central America, were spicing up the lives of Europe's elite with vanilla, chocolate, and tomatoes. After his visit to Peru, Christopher Columbus introduced both sweet and white potatoes and played an important role in the transportation and introduction of sugar. Eventually, these exciting new comestibles found their way through Europe and back to settlements in Florida.

While not recent discoveries from exotic new lands, there were plenty of foods common throughout Spain and Europe that were carried back to Florida aboard ships commanded by Juan Ponce, Hernando de Soto, and others from the Spanish fleet. With settlements in Cuba and Hispaniola [Dominican Republic and Haiti], there were frequent and necessary stopovers in these Caribbean ports. Inevitably, ships sailing to North America would end up transporting foods from Spain [which would include the culinary discoveries made by predecessors in other parts of the world], as well as ingredients readily available from the ports in which they stopped.

Of particular interest is the large number of ingredients, fruits, vegetables and livestock that the Spanish introduced to Florida in the 15th and 16th centuries. Much of the variety we take for granted today simply did not exist on North America before their arrival.

Florida enjoys a reputation today as a strong citrus producing state, and you would be forgiven for believing citrus is indigenous. When it comes to oranges, grapefruit, lemons, limes, and tangerines, these were all newly introduced to North America, via Florida, by the Spanish.

In the same manner, you would think ham and pork products were derived from pigs that were native to North American lands. While hogs were common throughout Europe, it was Columbus who first transported them from Spain to Cuba. Subsequently, animals from a growing Cuban herd were transported to Northeast Florida. It's no surprise that some of these animals escaped captivity and ran wild. Those that survived in the Florida wilderness are the ancestors to today's razorbacks.

Some of the other provisions that were moving around between ports and found their way to Florida include saffron, wine, rum, olive oil, bananas, figs, wheat, dates, almonds, quince paste, marzipan, hazelnuts, and peaches.

As with all of the European settlers who came to North America, the foodways of indigenous Indians influenced their culinary practices. It is known that, with exposure to foods prepared with corn, as well as cassava and other edible roots, the Spanish did not need to rely so heavily on imported wheat for making biscuits and bread. In addition, and while considered "desperation" fare, the Spanish recognized blackberries, acorns, certain tree leaves, and wild roots as locally available foods that could stave off hunger.

Just as the Indians influenced Spanish food preferences with locally grown fruits, grains and vegetables, the Spanish had a profound influence on the Indians. In particular, the peaches that arrived on Spanish ships were so broadly accepted and integrated into Indian life that observers considered peaches an indigenous fruit. The Indians also enjoyed pork, so much so that Spanish settlers used this meat as gifts and to keep the peace with local tribes.

While tomatoes did not make their way to Florida until much later, they were part of the agricultural treasure Columbus carried from Central America to Spain. Tomatoes were subsequently transported to Spanish colonies in the Caribbean where, as with many other foods, they found their way north into settlements along the First Coast.

With an abundance of foodstuffs being discovered, transported, introduced, experienced, and embraced around the world, the variety of foods available to settlement cooks was significant. Unfortunately, ingredients such as sugar, chocolate, and spices were terribly expensive and were enjoyed only by the wealthiest of families. For most of the settlers with meager incomes and limited resources, having enough food to ensure their survival was their primary concern. Naturally, they would rely on food they could hunt, raise on their properties, or purchase within their means.

While early settlers did not have access to the same variety of foodstuffs as did arrivals in the late 18th or early 19th centuries, there are many basics repeatedly mentioned in historic journals.

Some of the more familiar are:

BANANAS	KIDNEY BEANS	PORK
CASSAVA	LEMONS	RICE
CHESTNUTS	MULLBERRIES	SHRIMP
CRAB	OLIVES	SWEET POTATOES
FIGS	ORANGES	TANGERINES
GOAT	OYSTERS	TOMATOES
GRAPEFRUIT	PEACHES	WHEAT
GRAPES	POMEGRANATE	WINE

A survey of the Spanish culinary influence along the First Coast would not be complete without mentioning the datil pepper. For today's visitors, foods made or infused with datil peppers are commonplace. How the pepper actually got to this part of the world remains disputed.

In some reports, it is claimed that datil pepper plants were transported by the indentured servants [Minorcans] who traveled with the Spanish and populated early settlement communities. Others assert that traders carrying products from Cuba did not bring datil peppers to this region until the late 1880s.

Whatever the case, we know that Spanish culinary preferences leaned more towards foods that were sweeter and spicier than other nationalities. It is easy to see how ingredients such as the datil pepper, as well as bananas, tomatoes, peaches, sugar, and citrus would feature so prominently in the foods they prepared.

EMPANADIS [*See recipe - pg 31*]

FROMAJARDIS

Makes 12-16 *pastries* [*See Photo - Page* 30]

INGREDIENTS

DIRECTIONS

PASTRY
8 oz butter [two sticks]

6 oz cream cheese

2 C flour

1/2 tsp salt

1 egg [for wash]

1 T water [for wash]

FILLING
3/4 lb grated cheddar

1/8 tsp nutmeg

1/8 tsp cayenne

pinch salt

4 eggs - beaten

Preheat the oven to 350° F.

Beat the butter and cream cheese together. Add flour and salt and knead until the ingredients come together. Make four equal balls, cover and refrigerate for 15 minutes.

While the pastry is chilling, mix together the cheese, nutmeg, cayenne, salt and eggs.

Roll the pastry, one portion at a time, to a thickness of 1/16 inch. Cut into 4-inch circles. Place 1T of filling on one half of the circle, then fold over to make a half circle. Using a fork, pinch the dough closed, then place on a baking sheet. Using a toothpick, prick the top of each pastry, making 3-4 small holes that will allow steam to escape.

For the wash, beat together one egg and 1T water. Brush the top of each pastry with the wash.

Bake for 15-20 minutes until nicely browned.

SPICY RED BEAN SOUP

Serves 8

INGREDIENTS

DIRECTIONS

3 T butter

1/2 C onion, finely chopped

2 stalks celery, finely
chopped

1/2 C green bell pepper,
finely chopped

1 bay leaf

8 C water

1 1/2 C dry red beans

1 tsp brown sugar

1/4 C tomato puree

salt and pepper, to taste

Melt the butter in a large soup pot or Dutch oven. Sauté the onion,
celery, pepper and bay leaf until soft, about 10 minutes.

Add the water and bring to a boil. Add the beans, bring to a boil once
again, then reduce heat to a simmer. Continue cooking for about
1 1/2 hours, stirring frequently to avoid burning. If the soup gets too
thick, add water as needed.

Transfer the soup to a blender in small batches, puree, then return to
the pot. If you prefer whole beans in your soup, puree only half.

Add the sugar and tomato puree and simmer for another 30 minutes.
Add salt and pepper to taste.

Serve with warm, crusty bread.

THE FIRST COAST HERITAGE COOKBOOK

Spanish Settlers 1513 - 1821 • 32

ZESTY CRAB CUPS

Makes about 20 pieces   [*See Photo - Page* 34]

INGREDIENTS

....

2 T mayonnaise

1 birdseye [hot red] pepper, finely chopped

1 tsp lime juice

1/4 tsp salt

1/2 lb lump crabmeat*

2 large English cucumbers

1 T lime zest

DIRECTIONS

....

Whisk together the mayonnaise, pepper, lime juice and salt. Gently fold in the crabmeat, taking care not to break up the lumps. Set aside.

Peel the cucumbers, then cut into 1/2 inch thick slices. Using a small spoon, scoop out the center portion of each slice, creating a small bowl [take care not to break through all the way].

Fill each of the cucumber "bowls" with a teaspoon of the crabmeat mixture. Garnish with a pinch of the lime zest.

Refrigerate before serving.

....

* *When using lump crabmeat, always handle with care. Not only does lump meat taste great, the texture and overall appeal is enhanced when the larger lumps are kept whole.*

ZESTY CRAB CUPS [*See recipe - pg 33*]

LA FLORIDA STEW

Serves 10 - 12   [*See Photo - Page* 41]

INGREDIENTS

DIRECTIONS

3 T olive oil

2 T garlic, minced

3 1/2 lb boneless pork shoulder [Boston butt], cut into 2-inch pieces

2 tsp paprika

1 tsp red pepper flakes

1 tsp salt

3 C dry red wine

16 oz crushed tomatoes

1/2 C Kalamata olives, halved

zest of 1 orange

1 lb shrimp, large, cleaned

1 lb scallops

Pour oil in the bottom of a large Dutch oven. Add garlic and saute for one minute. Add pork, browning on all sides. Stir in paprika, pepper flakes and salt.

Cover meat with red wine [you can use more wine or simply add water] and bring to a boil. Reduce heat, cover and simmer for about 1 1/2 hours. Pork is properly cooked when it is easy to pull apart.

Blend in crushed tomatoes, olives and orange zest, then add the shrimp and scallops. Simmer, uncovered, until seafood is cooked through, about 10 minutes.

Serve with rice, broad noodles or thick slices of crusty bread.

ROAST PORK WITH PEACH SAUCE

Serves 8 - 12

ROAST PORK

3 lb pork loin

3 garlic cloves, cut lengthwise into slivers

1 tsp oregano

1/2 tsp cayenne

1 tsp salt

1/2 tsp black pepper

1/2 C fresh lime juice

1/2 C fresh orange juice

PEACH SAUCE

1 T butter

1 T shallot, finely diced

1 T flour

1/2 C white wine

2/3 C peach preserves

Preheat oven to 450° F.

Cut small knife slits all over the roast, then insert a slice of garlic into each.

In a small bowl, combine the oregano, cayenne, salt and pepper. Rub this spice mixture over the entire surface of the roast.

Place the roast in a pan, baste with juice mixture and place in the oven. After 45 minutes, and when the roast begins to brown, reduce heat to 350° F. Bake for an additional 1 hour or until the interior temperature of the roast reaches 160° F.

While the roast is baking, make the Peach Sauce.

Using low heat, melt the butter in a small saucepan. Add shallots and cook until soft, approximately 3-5 minutes.

Stir in flour to make a roux, cooking for another 3 minutes. Slowly add in the wine, whisk until thickened, then whisk in the preserves and salt.

When the roast is fully cooked, remove from the oven and allow it to rest for approximately 15 minutes. Slice and serve with Peach Sauce.

SHRIMP PILAU*

Serves 8 - 10

INGREDIENTS

3 T peanut oil

1 red onion, finely diced

2 medium carrots, finely diced

2 stalks celery, finely diced

4 cloves garlic, minced

2 ripe tomatoes, peeled and diced

2 bay leaves

2 C rice, uncooked

4 C fish stock

1 lb. shrimp, peeled and cleaned

salt and pepper, to taste

pepper sauce, to taste

DIRECTIONS

Heat the oil in a large sauté pan. Stir in onion, carrots, celery and garlic, cooking until soft, approximately 15 minutes.

Add the tomatoes and bay leaf, cooking for another 5 minutes. Add the uncooked rice and sauté a little longer. Add the stock, bring to boil, then cover and reduce to low heat, allowing the rice to cook for approximately 10 minutes. Add the shrimp, simmering for 10 minutes longer, until all of the liquid had been absorbed by the rice and the shrimp is fully cooked.

Add salt, pepper and pepper sauce, to taste.

 RICE DISHES MIGRATED AROUND EUROPE, CHANGING TO SUIT LOCAL PREFERENCES AND COOKING PRACTICES. PILAU [ALSO PILAF OR PAELLA] HAS CULINARY ROOTS IN FRANCE, SPAIN, AFRICA AND THE CARIBBEAN.

SHRIMP STEW

Serves 8 - 12

INGREDIENTS

DIRECTIONS

4 T butter

1 onion, finely diced

4 cloves garlic, minced

1 stalk celery, finely diced

2 T flour

1 1/2 C fish stock*

3/4 lb. tomatoes, coarsely chopped

1/2 tsp thyme

2 bay leaves

1/4 C parsley, finely chopped

2 lb. shrimp, cleaned

salt & pepper

Melt butter in the bottom of a Dutch oven or large sauté pan. Stir in onion, garlic and celery and sauté until soft but not browned.

Whisk in flour, a little at a time, to make a roux. Once incorporated, slowly add in fish stock, whisking to maintain a smooth consistency.

Stir in the tomatoes, thyme, bay leaf and parsley and simmer for 30 minutes.

Add shrimp and simmer for another 5-10 minutes, until fully cooked.

Add salt and pepper to taste.

Serve with thick slices of crusty bread or ladled over a scoop of rice.

* *A recipe for Fish Stock can be found on page 57.*

CLAM JUICE, FOUND IN MOST GROCERY STORES, IS A DELICIOUS AND CONVENIENT SUBSTITUTE FOR FISH STOCK.

CORN & BLACK BEAN SALAD

Serves 8

INGREDIENTS

1/2 C red onion, finely chopped

1 tsp garlic, pasted

1/4 tsp cumin

1 T lime juice

1 T molasses

1 T Dijon mustard

3 T olive oil

1/4 C orange juice

1 T orange zest

salt and pepper, to taste

2 C fresh corn

1 1/2 C black beans, fully cooked

1 red bell pepper, roasted and diced

DIRECTIONS

In a sauté pan, cook the onion and garlic until soft. Add the cumin and cook for one minute longer. Remove from heat and allow to cool.

Whisk the lime juice, molasses, mustard, oil, orange juice and orange zest together in a large bowl. Add salt and pepper, to taste. Add the onion mixture, corn, beans and bell pepper, mixing thoroughly. Cover and refrigerate overnight.

Taste and adjust seasonings just before serving.

ORANGE FRITTERS

Serves 2 - 4

INGREDIENTS

DIRECTIONS

1 egg

3 T sugar

1/2 tsp orange zest

1/2 tsp fresh orange juice

1/2 C ricotta

1/3 C flour

1/8 tsp salt

vegetable oil, for frying

confectioner's sugar, for dusting

In a large bowl, whisk together the egg and sugar until creamy, then add the zest, juice, ricotta, flour and salt.

Heat about a half inch of oil in a straight-walled pan. Drop the batter, 1 tablespoon at a time, into the hot oil and fry. When the bottom side is golden brown, flip the fritter and fry the other side.

When done, drain on paper towels. Dust with confectioner's sugar.

Best served hot.

THESE LITTLE GEMS PAY DELICIOUS HOMAGE TO THE SPANISH AND THEIR TRANSPORTATION OF ORANGES TO THE FIRST COAST.

LA FLORIDA STEW [*See recipe - pg 35*]

ROASTED ROOT VEGETABLES

Serves 8

INGREDIENTS

DIRECTIONS

1 lb carrots

1 lb turnips

1 lb sweet potatoes

4 T butter

2 T brown sugar

1/2 tsp nutmeg

1/4 C chicken stock

Preheat the oven to 400° F.

Peel the carrots, turnips and sweet potatoes, cut into 1 inch pieces and place in a large roasting pan.

In a small saucepan, melt the butter, then add the sugar, nutmeg and stock. Pour this mixture over the vegetables and toss.

Bake for approximately 1 hour, tossing the vegetables in the sauce every 20 minutes while baking. Vegetables are done when tender and nicely browned.

This recipe works well with any variety of firm root vegetable. Mix and match. Be daring and adventurous.

AUGUSTINES

Makes approximately 48 cookies

DOUGH

2 C flour

2 T sugar

1 tsp aniseed

1 lime, zested

1 1/2 C butter

1 T Pernod

ICING

1 C confectioner's sugar

2 T milk

1 tsp Pernod

DOUGH

Preheat oven to 350° F.

Pour the flour, sugar, aniseed and lime zest into a food processor and pulse together. Pulse in small pats of butter, a little at a time, until fully incorporated, then pulse in the Pernod.

Transfer the dough to a floured board and knead until smooth. Roll the dough into a ball, then cut into 4 pieces.

Roll each dough piece into a log shape and roll out to a thickness of 1/8 inch. Using a 2 inch round cookie cutter, cut dough into individual cookies and place on a greased baking sheet.

Bake cookies until firm - about 12 minutes. Transfer to wire rack and cool.

ICING

In a small bowl, combine the sugar, milk and Pernod until smooth.

Using a small spoon, drizzle the icing onto each cookie, until all of the cookies are covered. Allow time for drying, then serve.

DURING FESTIVALS IN ST. AUGUSTINE, BAKERS WOULD PEDDLE ROSQUETES THROUGHOUT TOWN. THESE DELICATE LITTLE COOKIES DERIVE THEIR FLAVOR FROM THESE FESTIVE SPANISH TREATS.

BANANA CREAM PIE

Serves 8

INGREDIENTS

DIRECTIONS

CRUST

2 1/2 C graham cracker crumbs

1/3 C sugar

1/4 C bananas, mashed

1/4 C butter, melted

FILLING

1 1/2 C heavy cream

1 1/2 C whole milk

3 egg yolks

1/2 C sugar

1/3 C cornstarch

1/4 t salt

2 T butter

1 t vanilla extract

5 bananas, ripe, sliced

TOPPING

Whipped cream

White chocolate shavings

Preheat the oven to 350° F.

For the crust: Combine the graham cracker crumbs, sugar, bananas and butter together until evenly mixed. Press this mixture into the bottom of a 10" oven-proof glass pie plate. Chill for 30 minutes, then bake for 15 minutes. The crust should be a pale golden color when done. Remove from oven and allow to cool.

For the filling: Whisk the cream, milk and egg yolks together in a heavy saucepan. Over medium-high heat, whisk in the sugar, cornstarch and salt, whisking constantly until the mixture thickens, taking care not to scorch or burn. When thick, whisk in butter and vanilla. Transfer the custard into a bowl and allow to cool.

To assemble, arrange half of the sliced bananas on the bottom of the pie. Pour half of the custard over top. Arrange a second layer of sliced bananas and custard to cover. Cover and refrigerate overnight.

To serve, top with whipped cream and shaved chocolate.

PEACHY WINE COOLERS

Serves 8 - 12

INGREDIENTS

....

2 T sugar

1 C Triple Sec *

750ml Viognier

3 peaches

1/4 C mint leaves [whole]

Garnish: orange slices
and/or mint leaves

DIRECTIONS

....

In a large pitcher, combine the sugar, Triple Sec and Viognier. Stir until the sugar is fully dissolved.

Peel the peaches, chop coarsely and add to the wine. Add the mint leaves and refrigerate for 4 - 6 hours.

Fill four wine glasses with ice. Using a strainer, pour an equal amount wine into each glass. Garnish with orange slices and/or additional mint leaves.

....

FOR A MORE INTENSE PEACH FLAVOR, TRY USING PEACH SCHNAPPS.

FRENCH SETTLERS

THE FRENCH FIRST EXPLORED THE MOUTH
OF THE ST. JOHNS RIVER IN 1562 [ORIGINALLY NAMED
THE RIVER MAY] AS PART OF A THREE-YEAR CAMPAIGN TO
SETTLE THE REGION AS FRENCH TERRITORY. AS YOU WILL
READ, THE RESULTS WERE LESS THAN FRUITFUL.

The French first set foot in Northeast Florida under the command of Captain Jean Ribault. While his visit was brief, it was long enough to spark controversy. The dispute stems from the fact that Juan Ponce had claimed La Florida as Spanish territory nearly 40 years earlier. When Ribault planted a stone marker declaring ownership of the territory, and subsequently naming it New France, he

was effectively trespassing on Spanish soil. The events that followed over the next three years would end in bloody defeat of the French and a less than graceful departure. But let's not spoil your appetite!

From a culinary perspective, indigenous Indians greeted Ribault happily, extended hospitality and welcomed the French explorers - more than likely with the ceremonial drinking of cassina and a meal of sofki.

According to Jacques Le Moyne, who traveled with Ribault, "[The Timucuans] brought us grains of roasted maize... smoked lizards or other wild animals... and various kinds of roots.

Some for foods, others for medicine. And when they discovered that we were more interested in metals and minerals, they gave us some of these as well."

Unfortunately, the planning of Ribault's crew left something to be desired. They were primarily a military attachment, did not know how to farm, and could not gather food effectively. Le Moyne continues "If the natives had not supplied us daily from their own stores, some of us certainly would have perished from starvation, especially those who did not know how to use a gun in the hunt."

It would take two more years and the arrival of Rene Laudonnièrre, along with his crew of 300 men and four women, before the French could potentially influence the foodways in northeast Florida.

The second French contingency, led by Laudonniere, arrived in 1564 to establish Fort Caroline near the marker that had been left by Ribault. While they carried sheep and chickens and other foodstuffs aboard their ships, they quickly ran out of supplies and found survival

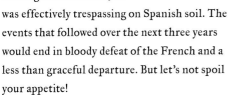

difficult. Through the generosity of the Timucua, this group of French settlers managed to survive. Their meals, not surprisingly, became much the same as those consumed by the Indians.

Some of the foods that the French learned to eat were locally sourced and introduced by the Indians.

Some of the more familiar are:

ACORN MEAL [FLOUR]	CORN	PLUMS
ALLIGATOR	CRABS	RASPBERRIES
BEANS	DATES	SHRIMP
BLUEBERRIES	FISH	SQUASH
CHICKEN	OYSTERS	TURKEY
COONTIE ROOT [FLOUR]	PERSIMMON	

Unfortunately, and over time, relations between the French and the Indians took a turn for the worse. Without the support of local tribes, the French diet also experienced difficulties. Facing starvation, historical records indicate that the French made interesting food choices. For example: soup made from chopped planks of wood pulled from the ship's floors; leather jackets and shoes boiled and served as meat replacements; stew made from newborn puppies; and, not surprisingly, one act of cannibalism. To say these settlers were desperate and hungry would be an understatement.

If there were any noteworthy culinary contributions made by these early French settlers, it would be the first Thanksgiving - a feast, shared with the Indians that took place shortly after their arrival to celebrate good fortune.

What's important to note is that this particular "Thanksgiving" was 57 years earlier than the one celebrated in Plymouth, Massachusetts - the event that gave rise to the gluttonous holiday now celebrated on the fourth Thursday in November throughout the United States. It goes without saying that when the French celebrated along the banks of the River May, their feast would have been quite different than the roasted turkey, glazed ham, prime rib, cranberry sauce, mashed potatoes, gravy, bread stuffing, green bean casserole, candied yams, pecan pie, and pumpkin pie that we enjoy today. It's important to remember that, during the mid- to-late 1500s, most of the ingredients necessary for such a feast were all but non-existent.

In 1565, a third fleet of French ships, commanded once again by Ribault, arrived to reinforce Fort Caroline. Had all gone according to plan, this would have allowed the settlement to thrive. Bad weather destroyed part of the fleet and Spanish attacks took care of the rest. The few French that survived sailed home without food, relying on hard tack biscuits and water en route.

It is important, however, to give the French some recognition for their culinary prowess. After all, in Europe they were creating trends, gaining recognition for their creativity, and were the darlings of the culinary world. In fact, throughout the 16th, 17th, and 18th centuries, the French were having the greatest influence on food preparation and culinary preferences throughout Europe.

In particular, the French were enjoying mutton, poultry, pork, and other meats, all served with sauces laden with garlic. Exotic and expensive spices were finding their way into recipes alongside ingredients such as anchovies, capers, and wine. The butter in France was considered the finest available and cheese was abundant.

A delightful quote from Brillat-Savarin, a French writer and food critic, provides a distinctly French perspective about cheese in the early 1800s: "A dessert course with no cheese is a beauty with only one eye."

Sugar and chocolate were also gaining popularity, although they tended to be so expensive that only royalty and the wealthiest of families could enjoy them. That being said, several French towns became famous for dragées [sugared almonds] and calissons [marzipan and crystallized fruits].

Another French specialty was spice bread, a cake made with either wheat or rye flour mixed with honey, cinnamon, nutmeg and cloves. Wafers made from a similar recipe were also popular.

What is amazingly clear and undeniably stunning is the sharp contrast between the culinary experiences that existed in France compared with the ones that took place in the settlement that failed to take root along the St. John's River. It goes without saying that, eventually, French culinary influences would find their way into American life and change the way we embrace food and its preparation. In the 1500s, however, and while the French explorers were on a quest for riches along the First Coast, things were dramatically different.

ST. JOHN'S CHICKEN SOUP

Serves 8

INGREDIENTS

4 T butter

1 1/2 C onion, finely chopped

1 1/2 C green pepper, finely chopped

1/2 lb ham, cut into 1/2 " dice

1 1/2 lb chicken breast, cut into 1/2" dice

6 C chicken stock

1 lb okra, trimmed, cut into 1/4" slices

28 oz tomatoes [canned], finely chopped

salt and pepper, to taste

Optional: 2-3 dashes hot sauce

DIRECTIONS

Melt the butter in the bottom of a large soup pot or Dutch oven. Stir in the onion and green pepper and sauté until soft.

Add the ham and continue cooking for about 5 minute. Add the chicken, cooking for an additional 5 minutes. Add the stock and bring to a boil, then simmer for 30 minutes.

Stir in the okra and tomatoes and simmer for another 30 minutes.

Add salt and pepper to taste and serve.

BAKED GARLIC SPREAD

Serves 8

INGREDIENTS

DIRECTIONS

3/4 C garlic cloves, peeled

3/4 C extra virgin olive oil

2 T butter

1 oz anchovy filets

Preheat the oven to 275° F.

Place all of the ingredients in a small baking dish. Cover and bake at for 1 1/2 hours, stirring every now and then to avoid burning. When done, the garlic will be soft and spreadable and the oil quite flavorful.

Serve with thick slices of crusty French bread.

IF YOU LOVE GARLIC, THIS DISH IS A KEEPER. YOU MAY, HOWEVER, WISH TO TURN ON THE EXHAUST FAN AND OPEN A FEW WINDOWS WHILE BAKING.

OYSTER BISQUE

Serves 8

INGREDIENTS

1 qt oysters

8 T butter [one stick]

1 C onion, finely chopped

2 celery ribs, finely chopped

2 bay leaves

1/4 C flour

2 C fish stock

1 C heavy cream

salt and white pepper,
to taste

2 T dry sherry

DIRECTIONS

Strain the oysters, reserving all of the liquid. Chop the oysters and set aside.

Melt the butter in the bottom of a large soup pot or Dutch oven. Over medium heat, stir in the onions, celery and bay leaves and sauté for about 5 minutes, until soft. Whisk in the flour to make a roux.

Slowly whisk in the stock and reserved oyster liquid. Bring to a boil, then reduce to a simmer and cook for about 20 minutes, whisking occasionally.

Transfer the soup to a blender, puree until smooth, then return to the pot.

Bring the soup to a boil once again, then reduce to a simmer. Add the cream and chopped oysters and cook for about 10 minutes.

Add salt and white pepper, to taste. Swirl in the sherry and serve.

SWEET CORN & TOMATO SALAD [*See recipe - pg 61*]

SMOKED FISH DIP

Serves 6 - 8

INGREDIENTS

DIRECTIONS

1/2 lb. smoked fish

1/3 C mayonnaise

1/3 C sour cream

2 T prepared horseradish*

For a smooth texture, place all of the ingredients together in a food processor and blend until smooth.

If you prefer to retain a little texture and evidence of the fish, do not use a food processor. Start by shredding or chopping the fish. In a separate bowl, whisk the mayonnaise, sour cream and horseradish together, then fold in the fish.

Refrigerate overnight so that the flavors can blend.

* Prepared horseradish is sold at most supermarkets and is typically found in, or near, the refrigerated dairy foods

CATFISH STEW

Serves 6

INGREDIENTS

4 T olive oil

2 onions, thinly sliced

8 garlic cloves, minced

6 red potatoes, peeled and cubed

2 lb catfish, cut into 1" pieces

1 C fish stock

1/2 C white wine

salt and pepper, to taste

1 lemon, juiced and zested

3 T flat-leaf parsley, finely chopped

DIRECTIONS

Heat the olive oil in a large Dutch oven. Add the onions and garlic, cooking over moderate heat until soft, about 5 minutes.

Add the potatoes, fish, stock and wine and bring to a boil. Reduce the heat and simmer, uncovered, for approximately 15 minutes, until the fish is fully cooked. Stir in the lemon juice and zest.

Ladle stew into bowls, garnish with parsley and serve.

IF THE NATIVES HAD NOT SUPPLIED US DAILY FROM THEIR OWN STORES, SOME OF US CERTAINLY WOULD HAVE PERISHED FROM STARVATION" *Jacques le Moyne*

CATFISH WITH CITRUS SAUCE

Serves 4

INGREDIENTS

4 Catfish filets

salt and pepper, to taste

4 T olive oil

4 T butter

4 cloves garlic, minced

2 T capers, drained

1 T flour

1 lemon, zested and juiced

2 T orange juice

1/4 C white wine

DIRECTIONS

Sprinkle salt and pepper on both sides of the fish filets.

Pour oil into the bottom of a straight walled sauté pan. When the oil is hot, place fish filets in the pan and cook for 5 minutes. Turn the fish once, cooking for an additional 5 minutes or until just cooked. Remove fish from pan and set aside.

Add butter to the same pan followed by the garlic and capers. Cook for 2 minutes. Whisk in the flour to make a roux. Slowly whisk in lemon juice, orange juice and white wine. If sauce becomes too thick, add more white wine.

Spoon sauce over fish, garnish with zest and serve.

SEAFOOD STEW

Serves 8 - 10

INGREDIENTS

2 T olive oil

1/4 C shallots, finely chopped

4 cloves garlic, minced

1 bulb fennel, quartered and thinly sliced

1 green pepper

4 C fish stock*

1 C dry white wine

2 C crushed tomatoes

2 tsp salt

1/2 tsp pepper

1/4 tsp red pepper

1/2 tsp basil

1/4 C fresh parsley, chopped

1/2 lb scallops

1/2 lb shrimp

1 lb catfish

2 T Pernod

1 lemon, zested

1 dozen clams [optional]

DIRECTIONS

Pour olive oil into the bottom of a large pot or Dutch oven. Using moderate heat, sauté shallots, garlic, fennel and green pepper for about 10 minutes or until soft.

Add stock, wine and tomatoes, bring to a boil, then cover and simmer for 30 minutes.

Add salt, pepper, red pepper, basil and parsley and simmer for an additional 15 minutes.

Add scallops, shrimp, catfish, Pernod and lemon zest and cook for 10 minutes. If using clams, add them as well and cook until their shells open [discard any clams that do not open].

To serve, ladle into bowls along with thick slices of crusty French bread.

* FISH STOCK
To make the fish stock, coarsely chop three onions, six carrots, 8 celery stalks and 1 bulb fennel. Put all of the vegetables, approximately 2-3 lbs. of fish bones and 3 bay leaves in a large soup pot and cover with enough water so that there is about 1 inch above everything. Bring to a boil, then simmer for 3 hours, adding more water as needed. When done, strain and discard the solids. The stock can be divided into small containers and frozen for future use. Makes approximately 8 - 10 cups of stock.

SHRIMP POT PIE [*See recipe - pg 59*]

SHRIMP POT PIE

Serves 8   [*See Photo - Page* 58]

INGREDIENTS	DIRECTIONS

SHRIMP FILLING

1 T butter

2 garlic cloves, minced

3 1/2 C sliced leeks

1/3 C dry white wine

2 C fish stock

1/2 lb potato, cut into
1/2 inch dice

1/4 tsp thyme

salt & pepper, to taste

1/2 C heavy cream

2 T flour

1 1/2 lb shrimp

**BUTTERMILK
BISCUITS**

2 C flour

1 tsp baking powder

1/2 tsp baking soda

1/2 tsp salt

1/2 C butter [cold, cut into
small pieces]

1 C buttermilk

Preheat the oven to 450° F.

To make the filling, melt the butter in the bottom of a deep, straight walled sauté pan or Dutch oven. Add garlic and leeks and sauté until tender, about 10 minutes. Add white wine and simmer until all of the liquid has evaporated. Add the fish stock, potatoes and thyme. Bring to a boil, then immediately reduce heat to a simmer, cooking until the potatoes are tender, approximately 10 minutes. Add salt & pepper to taste.

In a small bowl, whisk together the cream and flour. As soon as the potatoes are done, pour this mixture into the pot. Continue cooking until the sauce has thickened. Add the shrimp, simmer for another 3 minutes, then remove from heat.

To make the biscuits, mix the flour, baking powder, baking soda and salt together in a large bowl. Using a fork, cut in the butter until the flour is crumbly. Add the buttermilk to form a dough.

Roll the dough on a floured board to a 1/2 inch thickness. Using a cookie cutter, cut into 2 1/2 inch rounds.

Arrange the biscuits over the shrimp mixture. Place in the oven and bake, uncovered, for approximately 15 minutes or until the biscuits are golden brown.

CREAMY CORN SALAD

Serves 8 - 10

INGREDIENTS

3 T mayonnaise

3 T sour cream

1/4 C red bell pepper, finely chopped

1/4 C cilantro, finely chopped

2 tsp garlic, finely chopped

1/4 C green onions, coarsely chopped

4 C corn, freshly cut from the cob

1 lime, juiced

1/4 tsp salt

1/4 tsp black pepper

DIRECTIONS

Mix all of the ingredients together in a large bowl. Refrigerate overnight, then adjust seasoning as needed.

 CORN WAS INTRODUCED TO EUROPEANS IN THE EARLY 1500S, REPLACING MILLET IN SOME PARTS OF FRANCE.

SWEET CORN & TOMATO SALAD

Serves 10 - 12   [*See Photo - Page 53*]

INGREDIENTS

DIRECTIONS

2 lb. kernel corn

1 1/2 C tomatoes, diced

1/2 C red onion, sliced
razor thin

1 C green onion, finely
chopped

1 C cilantro, finely chopped

2 limes, juiced

1/3 C rice vinegar

salt, to taste

Mix the corn, tomatoes, red and green onions and cilantro together in a large bowl. Stir in the lime juice and rice vinegar. Add salt, to taste.

Refrigerate for 4-6 hours. Mix once again before serving, adjusting flavors as needed.

This dish goes great with grilled meats of all description.

BLUEBERRY JOHNNYCAKES

Serves 10

INGREDIENTS

2 c cornmeal

1C flour

1/2 C sugar

1 T baking powder

3/4 tsp salt

3 large eggs

1 1/2 C milk

1/2 C butter, melted

2 C frozen blueberries
[do not thaw]

maple syrup

DIRECTIONS

Preheat the oven to 400° F.

Grease the bottom and sides of a 13" x 9" baking pan with butter.

In a large bowl, whisk together the cornmeal, flour, sugar, baking powder and salt.

In a separate bowl, whisk together the eggs and milk.

Add the egg mixture to the dry ingredients, then add in the butter, mixing thoroughly.

Fold in the blueberries.

Bake for approximately 25 minutes or until a toothpick comes out clean from the center of the Johnnycake.

To serve, cut into squares and serve with warm maple syrup.

A DESSERT COURSE WITH NO CHEESE IS A BEAUTY WITH ONLY ONE EYE." *Brillat-Savarin*

FRENCH LACE COOKIES

Serves 8   [*See Photo - Page* 46]

INGREDIENTS

DIRECTIONS

9 T butter, melted

1 C brown sugar

1/4 C light corn syrup

1 T heavy cream

1 tsp vanilla extract

1/4 tsp salt

1/4 C flour

1 1/4 C rolled oats

1/2 cup pecans, chopped and toasted

Preheat oven to 350°F.

In a large bowl, combine the melted butter, brown sugar, corn syrup, cream, vanilla, and salt. Once the batter is fully mixed, add the flour followed by the oats and, lastly, the pecans.

Roll out parchment paper to fit your cookie sheet.

Place one teaspoon of batter onto the baking sheet, making sure to keep each spoonful a few inches apart from the next. Considering how the batter will spread [the resulting cookies are wafer thin], you may only be able to fit 5 or 6 cookies on a sheet.

Bake for 7 minutes. The cookies will be nicely browned and bubbling hot when done.

Remove the cookies from the oven. Transfer the parchment paper along with the hot cookies onto a cooling rack. After about 5 minutes, you will be able to transfer the cookies from the paper onto the rack for additional cooling.

Goes great with fresh sliced peaches and vanilla ice cream.

BEEF WITH MUSHROOMS [*See recipe - pg 72*]

BRITISH SETTLERS

FOLLOWING EARLIER CLAIMS BY THE SPANISH AND FRENCH, THE BRITISH DROPPED ANCHOR AND BEGAN COLONIZING NORTH AMERICA IN 1607.

They arrived in Florida with individuals trained in agricultural practices and with the resources to set up more enduring farming communities. While their first settlement in Jamestown, Virginia was situated further north and off of the Chesapeake Bay, they soon pursued territory to the south and into northeast Florida.

That being said, expansion did not take place without well documented conflict. It is clear, however, that the British understood the virtues of both patience and persistence and, in 1763, finally wrestled possession of Florida away from the Spanish.

Notably, the British did not rely upon or embrace Indian corn to the same extent as the French or Spanish. To them, corn was simply a grain used to feed livestock. It wasn't until they realized how much more reliable corn could be as an ingredient in their own culinary practices, as opposed to imported wheat, oats, or barley, that it became a steady part of their diet. Over time, corn found its way into British puddings, breads, and beer. It also appeared in recipes for succotash, grits, and hominy and was even enjoyed straight off the cob.

Even Benjamin Franklin became an advocate of corn, stating: "...Indian corn, take it for all in all, is one of the most agreeable and wholesome grains in the world... its green ears roasted are a delicacy beyond expression..."

In a similar manner, the British did not understand or appreciate hunting or fishing as a means of acquiring food. In England, these activities were considered diversions and nothing more. Not surprisingly, when British settlers first wrote about indigenous Indians hunting or fishing, they described them as being lazy.

Even the wild plums, most likely Chickasaw plums, enjoyed by indigenous tribes were shunned in favor of imported varieties that had been cultivated back home.

Ultimately, the British settlers stubbornly resisted the established foodways for many years, preferring to rely on long-held European culinary practices for survival.

With established trading routes supplying settlements to the North, transportation of vital and more familiar goods to the South allowed them to maintain these preferences.

Of course, the British did provide numerous, and delicious, contributions to the culinary landscape along the First Coast. Some of their more noteworthy include roasts of beef, lamb, and mutton as well as ingredients such as cherries, apples, white potatoes, and peas. These foods, which had been enormously popular in Britain, were transported to the northern colonies where British rule was confirmed. As the British gained control over Florida, these ingredients found their way into the region.

At the same time, and while the Spanish had already imported hogs from Hispaniola and Cuba into Florida, the British introduced European hogs. Additionally, and with an unrivaled preference for beef, they also transported and established herds of cattle.

While the Timucua were grilling meats over open fires, arguably the precursor to modern backyard barbeques, the British introduced the first barbeque rub - a delightful mixture of salt, pepper, molasses, and lemon juice. There is further evidence of their preference for beef. In the late 1700s, with the abundant supply of oysters, Beef and Oyster Sausages were served with corn bread.

It is interesting to note that, as sailors made their way to America, they would catch turtles along the way. Ultimately, turtle would become a regular ingredient amongst settlers as part of soups and stews.

Another curiosity is that, while the Spanish introduced both sweet and white potatoes to Europe, and Spanish fleets transported and introduced sweet potatoes to Hispaniola and onward to settlements in northeast Florida, the white potato took a much different route.

The white potatoes that traveled with Columbus and Spanish Conquistadores from Peru and Central America, along with sweet potatoes, made their way through Europe and into Britain. From there, British settlers, notably the Scottish and Irish, transported white potatoes into New Hampshire. Once there, white potatoes were carried southward, eventually making their way into British settlements in Florida.

Obviously, the British were much better established in northern settlements before making their way into the South. As such, they had gained access to a considerable variety of foodstuffs, both locally produced and imported from Europe.

It is interesting to note that, while French and Spanish cuisine in Europe was acknowledged as spicier and more flavorful, and many of these preferences influenced food preparation along the First Coast, British fare, in spite of the substantial variety of ingredients, was exceedingly bland.

When it came to the use of fruit, it was considered unhealthy in its raw state and responsible for inducing fevers. Accordingly, fruit was most likely to be associated with recipes that required cooking, such as stews, baked pies and tarts.

Some of the foods enjoyed by the British include:

APPLES	CUCUMBER	PEPPERCORNS
BACON	DUCK	PORK
BEANS	EGGPLANT	POTATOES
BEEF	EGGS	RAISINS
BEETS	GOOSE	SUGAR
BUTTER	LAMB	STRAWBERRIES
CABBAGE	MILK	TRIPE
CAULIFLOWER	NUTS	TURTLE
CELERY	ONIONS	TURNIPS
CHICKEN	PEAS	VENISON

At the same time, and with the increasing popularity of sugar in the 1700s and 1800s, the British are credited with having the "sweetest tooth in Europe." Accordingly, British desserts would include cakes, tarts, puddings, and assorted confections. Although many styles of ginger cakes were available throughout Europe, gingerbread was a common treat found amongst British settlements. Without fail, theses sweets eventually made their way into households throughout northeast Florida.

When it came to liquid accompaniments, British beverages [as with most drinks during this era] had some degree of alcohol content. Recognizing that the consumption of water could prove fatal [the presence of bacteria was not discovered until 1676 and not associated with disease until the 1800s], and that boiling [which killed bacteria] was involved in the making of ales and spirits, the British are remembered for the production and consumption of a large number of intoxicating brews including ale [beer], arrack [spirit], claret [wine], hard cider, hock [wine] , madeira [fortified wine], port [fortified wine], porter [beer] and rum [spirit].

Rum and the establishment of distilleries to produce rum was one of the more noteworthy contributions the British brought to the North American landscape. That being said, the rum that found its way to the First Coast was either transported south from the colonies or imported directly from distilleries in Cuba, Hispaniola, and/or other Caribbean nations.

In spite of Spain's reclamation of the territory in 1784, Florida became an American territory in 1821, ending Spanish rule in this region forever. Needless to say, the British influences remained, producing a lingering and undeniable impact on agriculture and culinary preferences along the First Coast.

BAKED OYSTERS

Serves 8

INGREDIENTS

2 T butter

2 T flour

1 C heavy cream

4 strips bacon, chopped

4 C leeks, sliced razor thin

1 C celery, finely chopped

1/4 C white wine

2 T Parmesan cheese, grated

salt & pepper, to taste

24 oysters, shucked

1 C breadcrumbs

NOTE: You will need 8 small ramekins to make this recipe.

DIRECTIONS

Preheat oven to 500° F.

Melt the butter in a small saucepan. Whisk in the flour and cook for 2 minutes. Slowly add the cream, whisking constantly. When somewhat thickened, remove from heat and set aside.

Using a large sauté pan, fry the bacon until soft, approximately 5 minutes. Add the leeks and celery and sauté until soft, about ten minutes longer. Stir in the wine and cook for 1 minute, then add the cream sauce and bring to simmer. Continue cooking over low heat until thickened. Add the Parmesan, followed by salt and pepper, to taste.

To prepare individual servings, place 2 - 3 oysters [depending on size] in the bottom of each of 8 ramekins. Cover the oysters with a small amount of leek mixture, then dust lightly with bread crumbs.

Bake until bubbly hot and browned, approximately 10 minutes. Serve immediately.

CORNBREAD MUFFINS

Serves 8

INGREDIENTS

2 C white rice, fully cooked

1 1/2 C corn meal

2 tsp baking powder

1 tsp salt

1 T butter, melted

3 large eggs

3/4 C whole milk

DIRECTIONS

Preheat the oven to 400° F.

Combine the rice, corn meal, baking powder and salt in a food processor until fully incorporated. Add the butter, eggs and milk and blend thoroughly.

Pour the batter into greased muffin cups and bake until lightly browned.

Serve warm with butter, whipped cream cheese, peach preserves and/or orange marmalade.

> BEER IS LIVING PROOF THAT GOD LOVES US AND WANTS US TO BE HAPPY."
> *Benjamin Franklin*

SHRIMP & CORN FRITTERS

Serves 8   [*See Photo - Page* 71]

INGREDIENTS

DIRECTIONS

1 C flour

1/2 tsp baking soda

1/2 tsp baking powder

3/4 C buttermilk

1 egg, separated

1 T butter, melted

1 lb shrimp, fully cooked, coarsely chopped

1 C corn kernels [fresh if available]

3 T green onion, finely chopped

salt & pepper, to taste

vegetable oil, for frying

1 lemon, cut into 8 wedges

Make the dipping sauce [below] in advance and refrigerate.

Pour one inch of oil into a high walled frying pan or Dutch oven and heat to 325° F.

Whisk together the flour, baking soda and baking powder followed by the buttermilk, egg yolk and butter. Mix in the shrimp, corn, onion, salt and pepper.

In a small bowl, whisk the egg white until stiff, then fold into the batter.

Place one heaping teaspoon of batter into the hot oil. Repeat until the pan is full, being careful you do not crowd the fritters. Allow one side to cook until golden brown, then turn. When fritters are fully cooked, place on a towel to drain, then transfer to a clean tray and keep warm in the oven at 350° F.

Serve with SPICY COCKTAIL SAUCE [page 19] and lemon wedges.

SHRIMP & CORN FRITTERS [*See recipe - pg 70*]

BEEF WITH MUSHROOMS

Serves 6 [*See Photo - Page 64*]

INGREDIENTS

DIRECTIONS

4 T olive oil

6 cloves garlic, minced

1 lb mushrooms, sliced

1 1/2 lb beef for stew,
cut into 1" cubes

1 C crushed tomatoes

1/2 C red wine

salt and pepper, to taste

Pour olive oil into a large Dutch oven. Over moderate heat, sauté the garlic briefly, then add the mushrooms. Stir and cook for about 5 minutes.

Add the beef, browning on all sides, cooking for about 5-10 minutes.

Add the crushed tomatoes, red wine, salt and pepper and cook for an additional 60 minutes or until beef is tender. If additional liquid is needed, use red wine.

Serve over buttered rice or noodles.

MUTTON STEW

Serves 8 - 10

INGREDIENTS

1/4 C olive oil

2 onions, roughly diced

4 garlic cloves, chopped

4 carrots, roughly diced

6 stalks celery, roughly diced

1 T fresh rosemary leaves, finely chopped

4 lb lamb, cut into 1" cubes

2 C red wine

1/2 C tomato paste

2 C vegetable stock [or water]

6 potatoes, diced

salt & pepper, to taste

DIRECTIONS

Pour oil into a large Dutch oven over medium heat. Add the onions, garlic, carrots, celery and rosemary and cook until the onions are translucent, about 5 minutes.

Add the lamb, cooking until the meat is fully browned on all sides. Add the wine and tomato paste and cook for 10 minutes. Add the stock and bring to a boil, then reduce to simmer and cook for 2-3 hours until the meat is tender. Check the pot, stirring occasionally, adding more water as needed.

Add the potatoes and cook for about 10 minutes longer, until the potatoes are tender. Season with salt and pepper to taste and serve.

ROASTED BEEF WITH GRAVY

Serves 8 - 10

INGREDIENTS

DIRECTIONS

1 C beef broth

3 lb. sirloin roast

10 cloves garlic, minced

2 T olive oil

2 tsp salt

2 tsp black pepper

2 teaspoons dried thyme

Place the beef broth in the bottom of a roasting pan [not much larger than the roast], then place the roast into the broth.

In a small bowl, mix together the garlic, olive oil, salt, pepper and thyme. Spread the mixture evenly over the top of the roast, allowing it to sit for about 1 hour, unrefrigerated.

Preheat the oven to 500° F.

Bake the roast for 15 minutes at 500° F, then reduce to 325° F. Continue roasting for approximately 20 minutes, checking for an internal temperature of 135 degrees [medium rare].

Remove from the oven and let rest, about 15 minutes, before slicing.

To make the gravy, transfer drippings to a small saucepan and bring to a simmer. In a separate container, whisk 1 T flour with 1/2 C water. Slowly pour the flour mixture through a strainer and into the saucepan, stirring constantly to avoid lumps. Cook gravy until thick, then immediately remove from heat and serve.

RED SKIN POTATO SALAD

Serves 8 - 10

INGREDIENTS

4 lb red potatoes

2 tsp sugar

4 T white wine vinegar

1/3 C shallot, finely chopped

2 T coarse Dijon mustard

2 T extra virgin olive oil

salt & pepper, to taste

DIRECTIONS

Wash the potatoes thoroughly. Since this recipe keeps the skin on, you want to be sure to remove all of the eyes and fibrous blemishes.

Cut the potatoes into large dice and place in a large pot. Cover with cold water and bring to a boil. Reduce the heat slightly and cook the potatoes for approximately 10 minutes. When done, drain completely, rinse with cold water and drain again. Set aside to cool.

In a large bowl, whisk together the sugar, vinegar, shallots, mustard and oil. Add salt and pepper to taste. Toss in the potatoes, making sure they are fully coated with the dressing. Refrigerate for 4 hours, or overnight, before serving.

SWEET POTATO MINI MUFFINS

Makes 24

INGREDIENTS

DIRECTIONS

1 C flour

2 tsp baking powder

1/2 tsp salt

1 tsp cinnamon

1/2 tsp nutmeg

1/4 C butter, softened

1/2 C sugar

3 eggs

1 C mashed sweet potato, fully cooked

2/3 C milk

1/2 C chopped pecans

Preheat oven to 400°F.

In a large bowl, whisk together the flour, baking powder, salt, cinnamon and nutmeg.

In a separate bowl, beat the butter and sugar until fluffy. Add the eggs, mashed potatoes and milk and beat until smooth. Fold the wet ingredients into the dry until completely incorporated. Stir in the pecans.

Pour the batter into greased mini-muffin cups and bake for 15 to 20 minutes or until a toothpick can be inserted and comes out clean.

Turn muffins onto a cooling rack. Best served warm.

ORANGE BREAD PUDDING

Serves 8

INGREDIENTS

DIRECTIONS

2 C milk

4 C bread cubes,
1/2" squares

2 eggs, beaten

1/2 C sugar

1 orange, zested

1/4 C orange juice

1/8 tsp salt

1 1/2 C marshmallows,
small

Preheat oven to 350°F.

In a large bowl, combine the milk and bread, allowing ingredients to soak for about 30 minutes.

In a separate bowl, whisk the egg and sugar until fluffy, then whisk in the orange zest, juice and salt.

Gently fold the orange mixture in with the bread, then pour into a greased 2 quart baking dish. Bake at 350°F for approximately 1 hour or until lightly browned. Remove the pudding from the oven, cover with marshmallows, then bake an additional 15 minutes or until the marshmallows are browned.

Serve warm with Orange Sauce [see below].

ORANGE SAUCE

Serves 8

INGREDIENTS

DIRECTIONS

1 C fresh orange juice

1 1/2 T cornstarch

2 T [1/4 stick] unsalted
butter

1/4 C sugar

1 T orange zest [1 orange]

1/4 C cream

In a small bowl, whisk the juice and cornstarch together, then add in the orange peel.

Separately, melt the butter in small saucepan. Over medium-high heat, whisk in the sugar, then add the orange juice mixture. Whisk constantly until sauce thickens. Remove from heat. Slowly whisk in the cream until a smooth texture is achieved.

ORANGE BUTTERCREAMS [*See recipe - pg 79*]

ORANGE BUTTERCREAMS

Serves 8   [*See Photo - Page* 78]

INGREDIENTS

2 T butter, softened

2 oz. cream cheese, softened

2 T orange juice

1 lb confectioner's sugar

1 tsp orange zest

2 C almonds, chopped

DIRECTIONS

Using a mixer, combine butter, cream cheese and orange juice. Beat in sugar and orange zest, a little at a time. Cover and refrigerate for 1 hour.

Place almonds in a low, flat dish. Roll buttercreams into small balls, then roll in almonds, coating completely.

To store, cover and refrigerate in a flat container.

For variety, substitute orange juice and zest with lemon or lime. You can also roll the buttercreams in other nuts and/or toasted coconut.

GINGERSNAPS

Makes approximately 24 cookies

INGREDIENTS

1/4 C butter, softened

1/4 C sugar

1 egg

1/4 C molasses

1 tsp ginger

1/4 tsp baking soda

1/8 tsp salt

1 1/2 C flour

DIRECTIONS

Preheat the oven to 350°F.

Using a mixer, combine the butter and sugar until creamy, then add the egg and molasses. Continue beating, adding the ginger, baking soda and salt. Add in the flour, a little at a time, until the flour is fully incorporated and a dough is formed.

Gently knead this dough on a floured surface, forming a ball. Cover with plastic wrap and chill overnight.

Roll out the dough on a floured surface to a thickness of 1/4 inch. Using whatever cookie cutter you prefer, cut and place cookies on greased baking sheets.

Bake for 10-15 minutes until lightly browned. Transfer cookies to a wire rack and allow to cool.

PEACH COBBLER

Serves 8

INGREDIENTS

DIRECTIONS

FILLING

6 C fresh peaches, peeled
and sliced

1/2 C sugar

1/4 C cornstarch

1 tsp lemon juice

1/4 tsp cinnamon

pinch nutmeg

TOPPING

1 1/2 C flour

1 1/2 tsp baking powder

1/2 tsp salt

2 T sugar

4 T butter, cut into small
pieces

1 egg

2/3 C milk

Preheat the oven to 425°F.

For the filling, mix the peaches, sugar, cornstarch, lemon juice, nutmeg
and cinnamon together in a large bowl. Once all of the ingredients are
fully combined, pour the mixture into a greased 9 x 13 baking dish.

For the topping, combine the flour, baking powder, salt and sugar in a
food processor. Add small pieces of butter, a little at a time, pulsing
to achieve a sandy texture.

In a separate bowl, combine the egg and milk and whisk together.
Gradually pour this egg mixture, a little at a time, into the flour,
pulsing as you go. The goal is to get a crumbly dough. Once this
texture is achieved, you can discard the remaining liquid. Spoon the
batter evenly across the surface of the fruit. Bake for 30-40 minutes
until the crust is nicely browned.

Goes great with peach and/or vanilla ice cream.

SYLLABUB

Serves 4

INGREDIENTS

zest of 1 lemon

2 lemons, juiced

1/4 C sherry

1/2 C white wine

1/4 C sugar

2 C heavy cream

DIRECTIONS

Before juicing, zest one of the lemons and reserve for garnish.

Whisk together the lemon juice, sherry, wine and sugar until the sugar is fully dissolved. In a separate bowl, whip the cream until stiff, then fold into the wine mixture. Cover and refrigerate overnight.

To serve, rim a martini glass with sugar, spoon in syllabub and garnish with lemon zest.

THIS IS A BEVERAGE THAT WAS SERVED THROUGHOUT COLONIAL AMERICA. AT FORMAL DINNERS, IT WAS SERVED JUST AFTER THE ROAST.

THE AFRICAN INFLUENCE DURING THE EARLIEST SETTLEMENT ALONG THE FIRST COAST WAS PROFOUND AND CONTINUES TO INFLUENCE THE SOCIAL, POLITICAL, AND CULINARY LANDSCAPE TODAY.

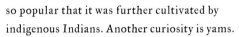

Historically, Africans were part of every Spanish expedition to Florida, including the 1492 voyage of Christopher Columbus and the 1513 voyage of Juan Ponce de Leon. Many were free men and women. Primarily, it was the British who brought enslaved Africans to North America beginning in the early 1700s.

From a culinary perspective, the African impact on food preparation and recipe development throughout the South produced a lasting and distinctive regional American cuisine.

The foods available along the First Coast were quite similar to those in Africa, allowing the Africans to rapidly embrace local ingredients as part of their daily diet. Additionally, since Africans rejected the unfamiliar white man's food provided on slave ships, transporters carried traditional African foodstuffs, including okra, watermelon, peanuts, yams, and several varieties of beans to ensure the survival of their human cargo.

It is interesting to note that during the earliest years of African settlement, watermelon became so popular that it was further cultivated by indigenous Indians. Another curiosity is yams. Growing up to three feet in length and weighing upwards of forty pounds, true yams were only found in Africa. The "yams" today are sweet potatoes discovered by Spanish explorers in Mesoamerica and subsequently brought to the First Coast.

Despite new surroundings and unfamiliar ingredients, African cooks were creative and quickly developed recipes that were uniquely their own. Additionally, some of the dishes resembled or were influenced by the meals prepared aboard slave ships, including Dab-a-Dab [a pulp of rice, beans, and yams], Flabber Sauce [palm oil, flour, water, and chili pepper], and Lob-lolly/Stirt-about [a thick soup made from cornmeal and potato].

Over time, a clearly distinctive set of African inspired culinary preferences and recipes emerged. They included new varieties of soups, stews, and one-pot meals, as well as a culinary regime much higher in vegetable content than any of the European diets.

AFRICAN INFLUENCE

The list of ingredients that can be linked to African settlers and slaves is extensive. As you can see,

Some of the more familiar are:

BANANAS	HICKORY NUTS	RICE
BEANS	MUSTARD GREENS	SEA TROUT
BEEF	LENTILS	SHRIMP
BLACK-EYED PEAS	MAIZE [CORNMEAL]	SORGHUM
CABBAGE	MOLASSES	SPINACH
CASSAVA	OKRA	SQUASH
CATFISH	OPOSSUM	SQUIRREL
CHESTNUTS	ORANGES	STONE CRAB
CHICKEN	OYSTERS	SWEET POTATOES
CHICKPEAS	PEAS	TURNIP
CHIVES	PLANTAINS	TURTLE
MALEGUETA PEPPERS	PORK	WALNUTS
COLLARD GREENS	PUMPKIN	WATERCRESS
CROAKER	RABBIT	WATERMELON
DEER	RACCOON	WILD GARLIC
EGGPLANT	RED PEPPER	YUCCA

While masters would introduce red meat, particularly beef, into the meals provided for African slaves, the better cuts, such as chops, steaks, and loins, were reserved for the "big house." It was the off-cuts and organ meats, including tongue, liver, intestines, heads, feet, and lungs, that found their way into slave cooking. According to an anonymous slave quote, slaves would use everything from the "rooter to the tooter." Meats, therefore, were used more for seasoning in dishes featuring vegetables or grains. One such example uses cabbage, collards, and other leafy greens combined with a little fatty meat for flavoring, boiled to make "pot likker" and eaten with cornbread.

When baking bread, cornmeal was preferred. Although wheat had been introduced and made popular by the British, Africans shunned it as a food of their masters. Accordingly, cornmeal found its way into spoonbread, hoecakes, and Johnnycakes, and also was used for grits, porridge, and as a thickener in soups and stews.

Africans also were known for their love of rich and spicy dishes using large amounts of salt, smoked meats, cayenne, hot chili peppers, and hot pepper sauces to make meals more flavorful. According to an African proverb, "The man who eats no pepper is weak; pepper is the staff of life."

While Africans cooked with palm oil and kola nut oil in their home countries, lard was much easier to find in the New World, contributing to a diet that included an array of fried foods. Nowadays, we associate African-inspired dishes such as fried chicken, corn fritters, fried catfish, and fried pork rinds with classic Southern foods.

It is known that indigenous Indians built wooden grill works over their fires and are given credit for the first backyard grills in northeast Florida. Subsequently, the Spanish followed with their own barbacoa. The Africans went one step further, refining this culinary practice with their roasted foods, frequently served with a barbeque sauce made from vinegar and peppers. As a matter of local interest, it has been noted that slave cabins at Kingsley Plantation near Jacksonville had brick fireplaces more than eight feet wide.

A discussion of African culinary contributions would not be complete without mention of groundnuts and peanuts. Originally transported by the Spanish from the Americas to Africa in the early 1500s, both were carried to North American by the Africans. In African cooking, groundnuts and/or peanuts were ground to a paste and used as thickeners in soups and stews. Ultimately, peanuts were easier to grow on plantations and literally took root in Southern foodways.

Here is a bit of trivia for those who have heard of Goobers [Nestlé's brand of chocolate covered peanuts]. The name is derived from the African name for groundnuts - nguba - and the original name for boiled peanuts in the South - Goober Peas.

Without the culinary influence from the Africans working in slave kitchens throughout the South during the 1500s, 1600s, and 1700s, it is unlikely that any of these marvelous foodways would have been created. While contemporary African cooking shares ingredients and cultural ancestry with Southern food preparation, it is entirely different. Undoubtedly, two of the most distinctive regional cuisines in America today are Southern Cooking and Soul Food, both owing their heritage to these early Africans.

PEANUT SOUP [*See recipe - pg 87*]

PEANUT SOUP

Serves 8   [*See Photo - Page* 86]

INGREDIENTS

4 T butter

1 medium onion, finely chopped

3 celery ribs, finely chopped

4 T flour

4 C chicken stock

1 1/2 C peanut butter

1/2 C dry sherry

2 tsp salt

1/2 C heavy cream

1/4 C dry roasted peanuts, chopped

salt & pepper, to taste

DIRECTIONS

Melt butter in a large pot. Add onion, celery and sauté until tender, approximately 3 to 5 minutes. Add flour, whisking until fully incorporated. Slowly add the stock, whisking constantly until smooth. Bring to a boil, reduce heat to simmer and cover, cooking for about 15 minutes. Transfer soup in small batches to a blender. Blend until smooth, then return to pot. Resume cooking over low heat, whisking in peanut butter, followed by sherry and salt. Add additional salt and pepper to taste.

To serve, ladle soup into bowls. Swirl in a little heavy cream and garnish with a sprinkle of peanuts.

POT LIKKER WITH DUMPLINGS

Serves 8

INGREDIENTS

POT LIKKER
1 large onion, quartered

2 carrots, coarsely chopped

2 celery ribs, coarsely chopped

2 heads garlic, halved horizontally

1/2 C fresh parsley, coarsely chopped

2 bay leaves

2 tsp salt

1 tsp peppercorns

1 lb collard greens, chopped

2 C turnip, cut into 1/2 inch cubes

2 C potato, cut into 1/2 inch cubes

DUMPLINGS
2 C flour

1 tsp salt

1 T baking powder

2 T vegetable shortening

3/4 C milk

DIRECTIONS

Place onion, carrot, celery, garlic, parsley, bay leaf, salt and peppercorns in a large stock pot. Add enough cold water to fully cover the vegetables by at least 1 inch and bring to a boil. Reduce heat and simmer for 1 1/2 hours. When done, strain all of the solids from stock and discard.

Add collards to stock, adding more water if needed, then cover and simmer for 30 minutes.

Add turnip and potato and cook for and additional 10 minutes, using more salt and pepper, as needed, to taste.

While the vegetables are cooking, make the dumplings. Sift the flour, salt and baking powder into a large bowl. Blend in shortening with a fork, then add milk, mixing well. Roll dough into a log and cut into 16 pieces. Roll each piece into a ball.

With likker simmering over medium heat, drop dough balls into the broth. Cover and cook for 15 minutes [do not lift lid] until done.

To serve, ladle likker, vegetables and two dumplings into each bowl.

CHICKEN & OKRA STEW

Serves 8   [*See Photo - Page* 92]

INGREDIENTS

4 slices bacon

1 large onion, diced

4 cloves garlic, minced

2 red peppers, diced

2 stalks celery, diced

1 lb boneless chicken, cut into 1" pieces

1/2 lb okra, sliced

1 lb tomatoes, chopped

1/4 tsp cayenne

4 C water, more if needed

salt & pepper, to taste

DIRECTIONS

Fry bacon in the bottom of a large Dutch oven. When cooked, remove from pan and allow to drain on paper towels. When dry, chop finely and set aside.

Using the bacon grease, sauté onions, garlic, peppers and celery for 10 minutes. Add reserved bacon, chicken, okra, tomatoes and cayenne and cook for 10 minutes more. Add water and bring to a boil, then reduce heat and simmer for 1 hour. Add salt and pepper to taste.

To serve, place a scoop of rice in the center of a large bowl. Ladle stew around the sides.

WHEN AFRICANS WORKED AS COOKS IN PLANTATIONS, THEY INTEGRATED NATIVE AFRICAN INGREDIENTS SUCH AS OKRA. THESE DISHES BECAME THE FOUNDATION FOR TODAY'S SOUTHERN CUISINE.

FRIED CHICKEN

Serves 6 to 8

INGREDIENTS

DIRECTIONS

4 chicken breasts [skinless and boneless]

1 qt buttermilk

2 C flour

1 T salt

2 tsp garlic powder

1 T black pepper

2 tsp paprika [sweet Hungarian]

1 tsp. ground thyme

Vegetable oil [for frying]

Cut chicken breasts lengthwise into three pieces and place in large bowl. Pour enough buttermilk into the bowl to cover chicken completely. Cover, place in refrigerator and marinate for 4 hours [Do not marinate longer - chicken may become mushy].

In a separate bowl, whisk together the flour, salt, garlic powder, pepper, paprika and thyme, making sure ingredients are thoroughly blended.

Use two hands, one for wet chicken pieces going into the bowl and one for floured pieces coming out of the bowl. Using your "wet" hand, take one piece of chicken from the marinate and place into flour mixture. Using your "dry" hand, cover the piece with flour, then turn, making sure to coat chicken strips evenly on all sides. Place the floured chicken pieces on a large platter or cookie pan. Repeat this process until all chicken is floured. Allow coated chicken pieces to dry for at least 30 minutes before cooking.

Pour enough oil into a high walled frying pan to reach a depth of 1/2 inch. Bring oil to 350° F. Using tongs, place chicken into the hot oil, cooking fully, one side at a time, until golden brown on all sides. Remove chicken from pan and place on paper towels to drain.

Before cooking a second batch, check temperature of oil, making sure it is always at 350 degrees.

Fry all of the chicken, keeping completed pieces warm in the oven.

Bring even more African heritage to the plate. Serve with Sweet Potato Salad [page 96] and Traditional Coleslaw [page 98].

PEPPER POT

Serves 8

INGREDIENTS

3 slices bacon, diced

1/2 C onion, finely chopped

1/2 C celery, finely chopped

2 leeks, finely chopped

2 green bell peppers, diced

1 C parsley, finely chopped

1 lb beef [for stew], cut into 1/2 inch cubes

6 C beef stock

4 T tomato paste

1/4 tsp dried thyme

1/2 tsp dried marjoram

1/2 tsp ground cloves

1 bay leaf

1 tsp black pepper

2 C potato, cubed

2 C carrot, diced

4 tablespoons all-purpose flour

1/4 C water

DIRECTIONS

In a large soup pot or Dutch oven, fry the bacon for 2 minutes. Add the onion, celery, leeks, green peppers and parsley and continue cooking until soft, approximately 5 minutes.

Add the beef, beef stock, tomato paste, thyme, marjoram, cloves, bay leaf, and black pepper. Bring to a boil, then simmer, uncovered, for 1 hour.

When the meat is tender, add the potatoes and carrots and cook for 20 minutes longer.

To thicken the broth, mix the flour with water, making sure all lumps have been worked out. Pour this mixture through a strainer into the pot and stir.

CHICKEN & OKRA STEW [*See recipe - pg 89*]

LIMPIN SUSAN

Serves 8

INGREDIENTS

4 strips bacon

1/2 lb. okra, cut into
1/4 inch slices

2 C chicken broth*

1 C uncooked rice

salt & pepper to taste

DIRECTIONS

Using a deep sauté pan, fry the bacon over moderate heat until nearly crisp. Add the okra and cook for an additional 5 minutes, or until just tender. Stir in the rice, thoroughly mixing in all of the grains. Pour in the stock and mix, allowing the mixture to come to a boil. Cover the pot, reducing the heat and simmer until rice is fully cooked - approximately 20 minutes. Add salt and pepper to taste and serve.

THE FLAVOR OF THIS DISH CAN VARY, DEPENDING ON THE STOCK YOU SELECT. RECOGNIZING THAT SUPERMARKET BRANDS TEND TO BE LOW IN FLAVOR, A RICHER HOMEMADE STOCK IS RECOMMENDED.

BUTTERMILK CORNBREAD

Serves 8

INGREDIENTS	DIRECTIONS

INGREDIENTS

4 strips bacon

1 C cornmeal

1 C flour

1/3 C sugar

1 1/2 tsp baking powder

1/4 tsp salt

1 C buttermilk

6 T melted butter

2 eggs, beaten

2 C fresh corn kernels

DIRECTIONS

Preheat the oven to 400° F.

Fry the bacon until crispy, drain on paper towels and crumble.

In a large bowl, whisk together the cornmeal, flour, sugar, baking powder and salt. Mix in the buttermilk, butter, eggs, corn and bacon.

Pour the batter into a greased, 2 qt baking dish and bake for 25 minutes or until lightly browned.

Optional: Use 1/4 C diced red bell pepper and/or 1/4 C fresh chopped cilantro instead of the bacon.

COLLARD GREENS

Serves 8

INGREDIENTS

1 lb fresh collards, coarsely chopped

4 strips of bacon, diced

1 large onion, peeled and diced

2 teaspoons salt

hot sauce, to taste

DIRECTIONS

Cook the bacon in a large stockpot until the fat is rendered. Add the onion and cook until translucent and soft.

Add the collards, mixing with the bacon fat and onions, and cook for 5 minutes.

Add just enough cold water to cover, bring to a boil, then cover and reduce to a simmer. Cook for 60-90 minutes until desired tenderness is achieved.

Mix in a few dashes of hot sauce, to taste and serve.

> THE MAN WHO EATS NO PEPPER IS WEAK;
> PEPPER IS THE STAFF OF LIFE.
> *African Proverb*

SWEET POTATO SALAD

Serves 8   [*See Photo - Page* 97]

INGREDIENTS

2 lb. sweet potato, peeled, cut into 1/2" cubes

1 T lemon juice

1 rib celery, thinly sliced

1 small Granny Smith apple, peeled, cut into 1/4" cubes

3 oranges, cut into "supremes"

1/4 C pecans, coarsely chopped

1 C mayonnaise

salt & pepper, to taste

DIRECTIONS

Place the potatoes in a large saucepan. Cover with water and bring to a boil. Reduce heat to a simmer until cooked, but still firm - about 10 minutes. Drain thoroughly, place in a large bowl, toss with lemon juice and allow to cool.

In a separate bowl, mix celery, apple, orange "supremes," pecans and mayonnaise. Toss mixture with cooled potatoes. Sprinkle with salt and pepper, to taste.

Perfect for summer picnics and outdoor parties.

TRUE YAMS, AVAILABLE ONLY IN AFRICA, GROW UP TO THREE FEET IN LENGTH AND CAN WEIGH UP TO FORTY POUNDS. THE "YAMS" AVAILABLE TODAY ARE ACTUALLY SWEET POTATOES FIRST INTRODUCED BY THE SPANISH.

SWEET POTATO SALAD [*See recipe - pg 96*]

TRADITIONAL COLESLAW

Serves 12

INGREDIENTS

1 head cabbage, thinly sliced

1 onion, thinly sliced

1 green pepper, thinly sliced

1 C vinegar

3/4 C peanut oil

1 T salt

1 T celery seed

1 tsp dry mustard

3/4 C sugar

DIRECTIONS

Using a food processor with a thin slicing blade, shred cabbage, onion and green pepper. When finished, transfer all of the vegetables to a large mixing bowl.

Combine vinegar, oil, salt, celery seed and dry mustard in a saucepan and bring to a boil. Remove from heat, add sugar and stir until completely dissolved. Pour mixture over vegetables and toss. Place the coleslaw in the refrigerator and marinate overnight. Toss before serving.

Slaw will keep up to two weeks in the refrigerator.

Goes great with grilled meats, especially pulled pork sandwiches.

SWEET POTATO PIE

Serves 8

INGREDIENTS

DIRECTIONS

FILLING

1 1/2 C sweet potatoes,
cooked and mashed

2/3 C sugar

2 T butter, melted

1/4 tsp mace

1/4 tsp cinnamon

1/2 tsp vanilla

1/2 tsp salt

2 T lemon juice

2 eggs, beaten

1 C heavy cream

PIE CRUST

1/2 C less 1 T shortening
[Crisco]

3 T boiling water

1 tsp milk

1/2 tsp salt

1 1/4 C flour, sifted

Preheat the oven to 375° F.

In a large bowl, whisk together the potatoes, sugar, butter, mace, cinnamon, vanilla, salt, lemon juice, eggs and cream until smooth.

To make the crust, put the shortening in a large bowl. Add boiling water and milk and, with a fork, cut and mix the ingredients until most of the liquid has been absorbed. Mix in the flour and salt until you can form a ball with your hands.

Roll out the pie crust and place in the bottom of a 9" pie plate, allowing about a 1/2" of dough extra all around. Roll the extra dough under the rim of the pie plate to make a crust edge. Pour the filling into the crust and bake for approximately 40 minutes, or until a toothpick poked into the center of the pie comes out clean.

Cool before serving.

Serve with vanilla ice cream, whipped cream or both!

PERSIMMON PUDDING

Serves 4

INGREDIENTS

....

1 1/2 C persimmon puree
[2 - 3 persimmons]

2 eggs, beaten

1/3 C sugar

1/2 C buttermilk

1/4 C cream

1 T honey

4 T butter, melted

1/2 C flour

1 tsp baking powder

1/8 tsp salt

1/2 tsp cinnamon

DIRECTIONS

....

Preheat oven to 350° F.

Wash, dry and peel persimmons, then cut into quarters. Using a food processor, pulse the fruit to make at least 1 1/2 C of puree.

In a large bowl, whisk together the eggs and sugar. Add the buttermilk, cream, honey and butter. Gradually whisk in the flour, baking powder, salt and cinnamon followed by the persimmon.

Arrange four, 1-cup ramekins on a baking sheet. Fill each with an equal amount of the batter, then bake for 1 hour. Remove from oven, allowing puddings to stand for up to 10 minutes before serving.

Puddings are even better topped with whipped cream or vanilla ice cream.

....

This recipe originally called for the American Persimmon. Depending on availability, you can also use the Japanese Hachiya or Fuyu varieties.

RECIPE INDEX

CATEGORY	RECIPE	
SIDES & SALADS	Buttermilk Cornbread	page 94
	Collard Greens	page 95
	Corn & Black Bean Salad	page 39
	Crab & Swamp Cabbage Salad	page 21
	Creamy Corn Salad	page 60
	Limpin Susan	page 93
	Orange Fritters	page 40
	Orange Sauce	page 77
	Red Skin Potato Salad	page 75
	Roasted Root Vegetables	page 42
	Spicy Cocktail Sauce	page 19
	Sweet Corn & Tomato Salad	page 61
	Sweet Potato Mini Muffins	page 76
	Sweet Potato Salad	page 96
	Timucua Salad	page 23
	Traditional Coleslaw	page 98
DESSERTS	Augustines	page 43
	Banana Cream Pie	page 44
	Blueberry Johnnycakes	page 62
	Corn Pudding	page 24
	French Lace Cookies	page 63
	Gingersnaps	page 80
	Muscadine Cheese Cake	page 25
	Orange Bread Pudding	page 77
	Orange Buttercreams	page 79
	Peach Cobbler	page 81
	Peach Pie	page 26
	Persimmon Pudding	page 100
	Sweet Potato Pie	page 99
BEVERAGES	Peachy Wine Coolers	page 45
	Syllabub	page 82

REFERENCES

An A to Z of Food and Drink
John Ayto
2002 Oxford University Press

Black Society in Spanish Florida
Jane Landers
1999 University of Illinois Press

Cambridge World History of Food
Kenneth F. Kiple, Kriemhild Coneè Ornelas
2000 Cambridge University Press

Chasing Chiles
Kurt Friese, Kraig Kraft and Gary Nabhan
2011 Chelsea Green Publishing

The Dictionary of American Food and Drink
John F. Mariani
1983 Ticknor & Fields

Florida Heritage Cookbook
Marina Polvay & Marilyn Fellman
1976 Florida Consultation and Management Inc.

Florida's First People
Robin C. Brown
1994 Pineapple Press

The Founders of American Cuisine
Harry Huff
2011 McFarland & Company

The Founding Foodies
Dave DeWitt
2010 Sourcebooks

High on the Hog: A Culinary Journey from
Africa to America
Jessica B. Harris
2011 Bloomsbury USA

A History of Horticulture in America to 1860
U. P. Hedrick
1950 Oxford University Press

Hog and Hominy: Soul Food from Africa to
America
Frederick Douglass Opie
2008 Columbia University Press

The Odyssey of an African Slave
Sitiki, Edited by Patricia C. Griffin
2009 University Press of Florida

The Oldest City - St. Augustine - Saga of Survival
Edited by Jean Parker Waterbury
1983 St. Augustine Historical Society

Oxford Companion to Food
Alan Davidson
1999 Oxford University Press

Oxford Encyclopedia of Food and Drink in America
Andrew F. Smith
2004 Oxford University Press

Slavery in Florida
Larry Eugene Rivers
2000 University Press of Florida

A Taste for War
William C Davis
2003 Stackpole Books

Three Voyages
Rene Laudonniere
2001 The University of Alabama Press

Under Five Flags
Jefferson Bell
1993 Special Publications Inc.

What the Slaves Ate
Herbert C. Covey and Dwight Eisnach
2009 Greenwood Press

SPECIAL THANKS

This book would not have been possible without the support of my friends, family, colleagues and a generous number of history and culinary specialists who live and work in and around the First Coast.

In particular, I'd like to thank Elizabeth Naab for her expert writing and editorial skills, Patrick Carter for his amazing design input, Vince Lupo for his keen photographic eye, Terry Rankin and James Kail for way too many things to list here and Jan Pilant for her digital prowess.

I'd also like to thank Jennifer Zuberer and Lucy Coward at the City of St. Augustine, the researchers and librarians at the Library of Congress, the Jamestown Yorktown Foundation, the St. Augustine Historical Society, the Hillsborough County Public Library and especially the staff at the Jacksonville Public Library.

I must also thank Louis and Hortense Spear as well as Richard Spear and Susan Poor. It is their unwavering love and support that has allowed me to pursue my dreams.